David Chen and his Partners

EDSA (Asian)

Classical Collection of Landscape in Line Drawings

Edited by   Long zhiwei   Hu yanli

EDSA (Asian) Classical Collection of Landscape in Line Drawings

First published in Chinese edition in 2005 by:
Shanglin A&C Limited©
Unit D, 10/F, China Overseas Building,
139 Hennessy Road, Wanchai, Hong Kong
Tel: +852-2972 9731
Fax: +852-2527 3298
E-mail: hk-shanglin@126.com
www.hk-sl.com

First published in English edition in 2005 by:
AZUR Corporation©
5F Aikusu Building,1-44-8,Jimbo-cho,Kanda,Chiyoda-ku,Tokyo 101-0051 Japan
Tel: +81-3-3292-7601
Fax: +81-3-3292-7602
E-mail: azur@galaxy.ocn.ne.jp

Distributors: AZUR Corporation
                5F Aikusu Building,1-44-8,Jimbo-cho,Kanda,Chiyoda-ku,
                Tokyo 101-0051 Japan
                Tel: +81-3-3292-7601
                Fax: +81-3-3292-7602
                E-mail: azur@galaxy.ocn.ne.jp

                Beijing Designer Books Co.,Ltd.
                Building No.2,Desheng Office Building,3Babukou,Gulouxidajie,
                Xicheng District, Beijing, China
                Tel: +81-10-6406-7653
                Fax: +81-10-6406-0931
                E-mail: info@designerbooks.net
                www.designerbooks.net

ISBN: 4-903233-05-7 C3052

Printed in China

CONTENTS

6-47 Plan View

48-117 Facade View

118-282 Perspective View

EDSA (Asian)

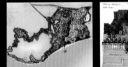

Plan View

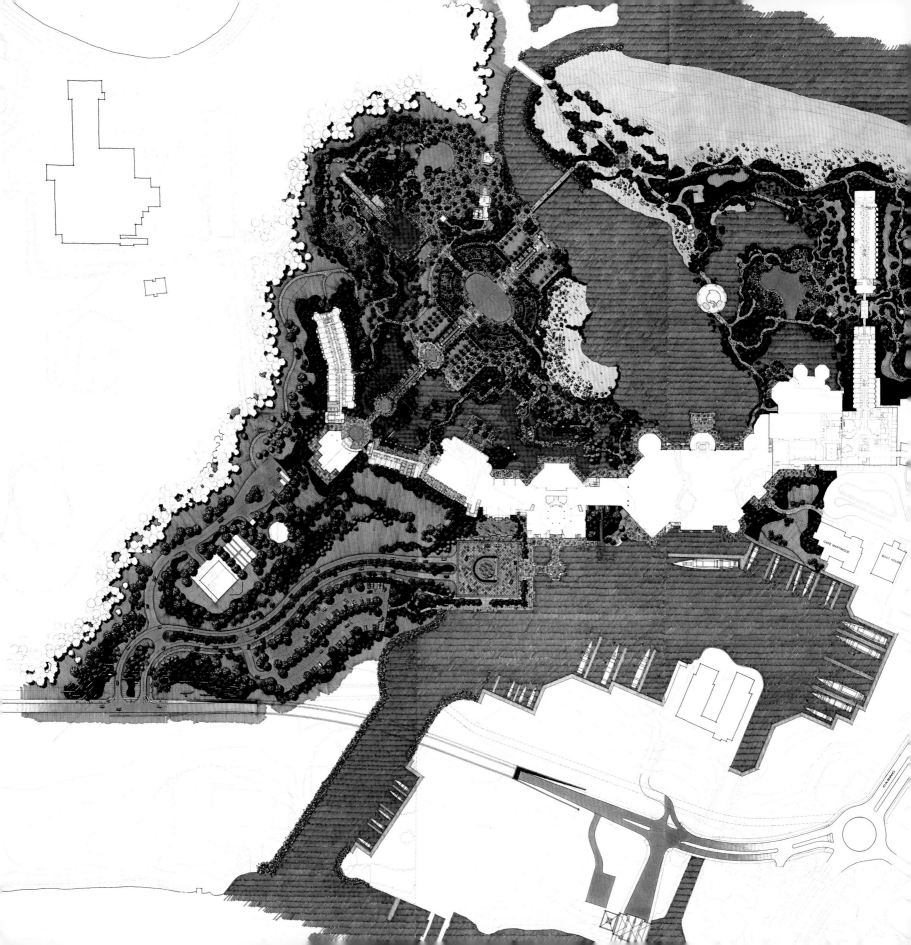

CAFE MARTINIQUE

BOAT HOUSE

CASINO

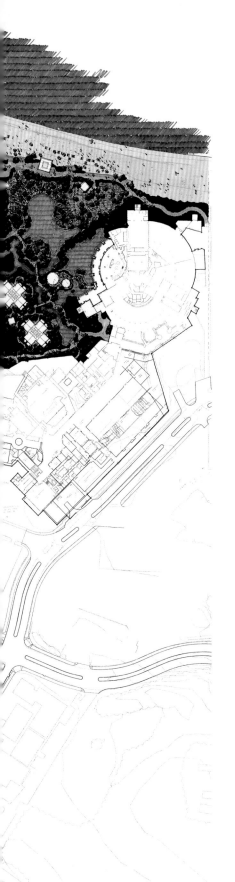

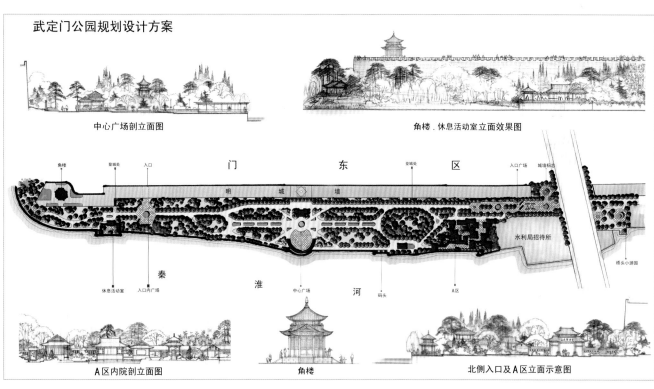

武定门公园规划设计方案

中心广场剖立面图

角楼.休息活动室立面效果图

角楼 登城处 入口 门 东 区 登城处 入口广场 城墙码头

明 城 墙

水利局招待所

休息活动室 入口内广场 秦 淮 河 中心广场 码头 A区 桥头小游园

A区内院剖立面图

角楼

北侧入口及A区立面示意图

Left: Bahamas Atlantis Holiday Resort. The key part is described detailedly, which, together with coating on a large scale, makes the whole picture conspicuous.
Line + Mark
Right: Nanjing Wudingmen Park. The facade view, using a technique like Chinese painting, tries to express a classical atmosphere.
Line + Mark + Color pencil

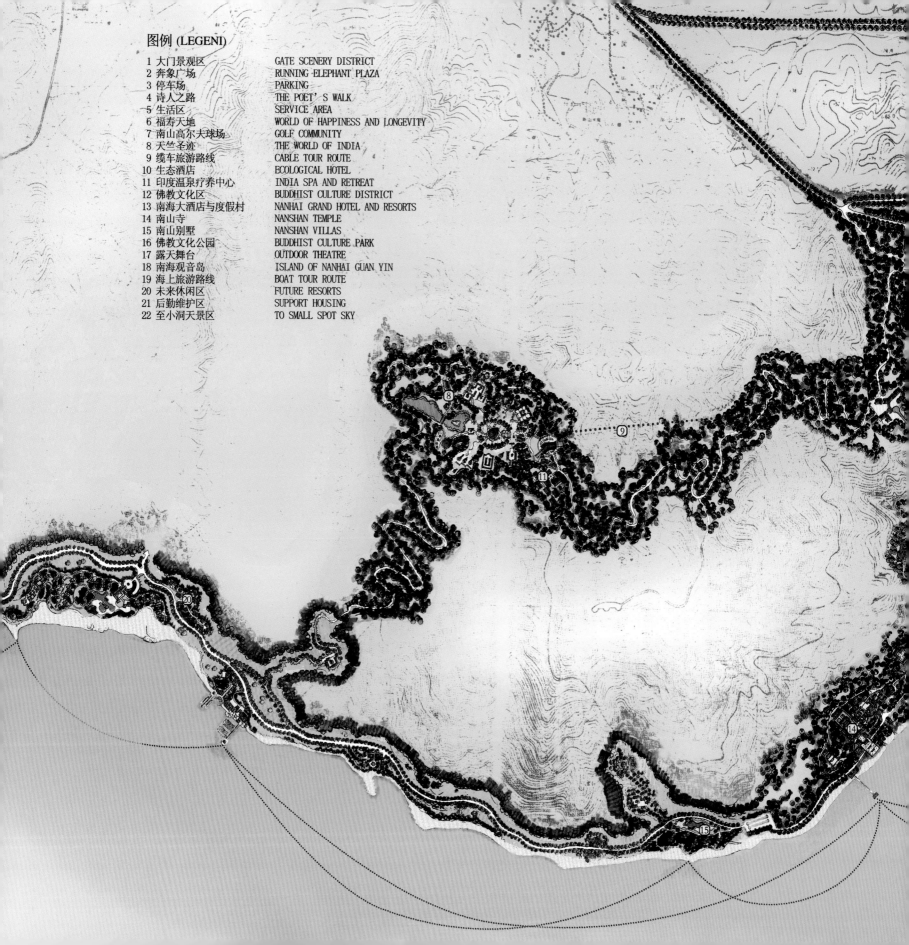

图例 (LEGENI)

1 大门景观区 — GATE SCENERY DISTRICT
2 奔象广场 — RUNNING ELEPHANT PLAZA
3 停车场 — PARKING
4 诗人之路 — THE POET'S WALK
5 生活区 — SERVICE AREA
6 福寿天地 — WORLD OF HAPPINESS AND LONGEVITY
7 南山高尔夫球场 — GOLF COMMUNITY
8 天竺圣迹 — THE WORLD OF INDIA
9 缆车旅游路线 — CABLE TOUR ROUTE
10 生态酒店 — ECOLOGICAL HOTEL
11 印度温泉疗养中心 — INDIA SPA AND RETREAT
12 佛教文化区 — BUDDHIST CULTURE DISTRICT
13 南海大酒店与度假村 — NANHAI GRAND HOTEL AND RESORTS
14 南山寺 — NANSHAN TEMPLE
15 南山别墅 — NANSHAN VILLAS
16 佛教文化公园 — BUDDHIST CULTURE PARK
17 露天舞台 — OUTDOOR THEATRE
18 南海观音岛 — ISLAND OF NANHAI GUAN YIN
19 海上旅游路线 — BOAT TOUR ROUTE
20 未来休闲区 — FUTURE RESORTS
21 后勤维护区 — SUPPORT HOUSING
22 至小洞天景区 — TO SMALL SPOT SKY

South Hill Culture Tourist Region (Hainan)
Line + Mark

11

Top: Part scheme. It builds a scale-pleasant and changeful port square, and the easy brushwork herein is of great advantage to express an amicable atmosphere.
Line + Mark
Below: Malaysia Miri Marina Park. The concise colouring herein makes the structure of the scheme clear and apparent.
Line + Mark

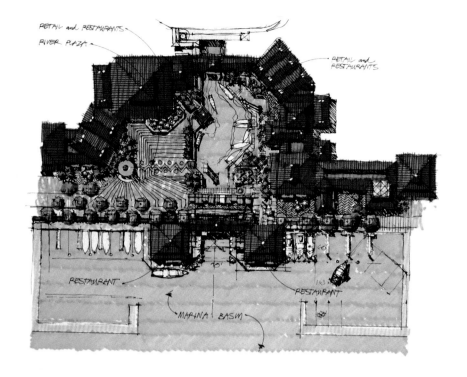

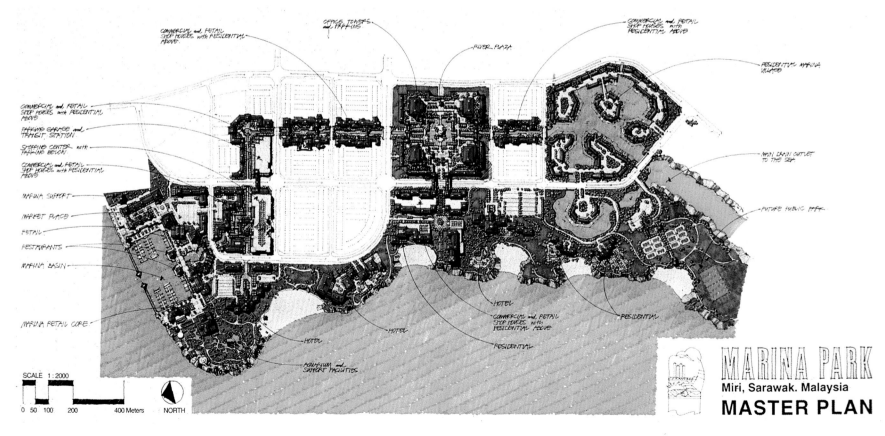

SCALE 1:2000

0 50 100   200   400 Meters   NORTH

MARINA PARK
Miri, Sarawak. Malaysia
MASTER PLAN

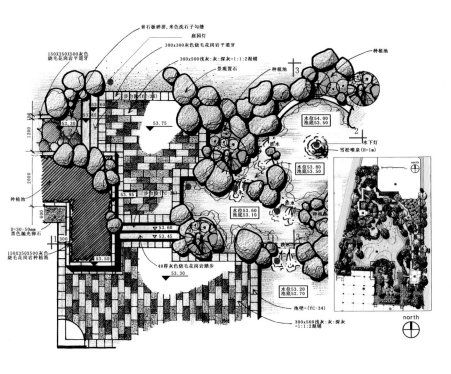

青石板碎拼, 米色洗石子勾缝
庭园灯
300x300灰色烧毛花岗岩平道牙
300x500浅灰:深灰=1:1:2混铺
景观置石
种植池
150X350X500灰色
烧毛花岗岩平道牙
种植池

水位54.00
池底53.50

雪松喷泉(H=1m)
水下灯

水位53.80
池底53.50

种植池
种植池

水位53.60
池底53.10

D=30-50mm
黑色抛光卵石
150X350X500灰色
烧毛花岗岩种植池

40厚灰色烧毛花岗岩踏步
53.30

水位53.20
池底52.70

池壁=(YC-34)

300x500浅灰:深灰
=1:1:2混铺

north

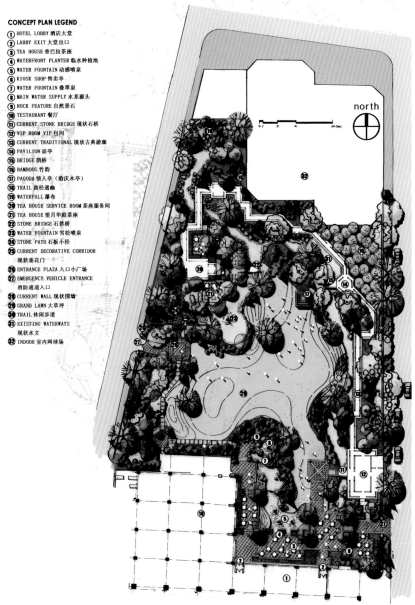

CONCEPT PLAN LEGEND

① HOTEL LOBBY 酒店大堂
② LABBY EXIT 大堂出口
③ TEA HOUSE 香巴拉茶座
④ WATERFRONT PLANTER 临水种植池
⑤ WATER FOUNTAIN 动感喷泉
⑥ KIOSK SHOP 售卖亭
⑦ WATER FOUNTAIN 叠翠泉
⑧ MAIN WATER SUPPLY 水系源头
⑨ ROCK FEATURE 自然景石
⑩ TESTAURANT 餐厅
⑪ CURRENT STONE BRIDGE 现状石桥
⑫ VIP ROOM VIP 包间
⑬ CURRENT TRADITIONAL 现状古典游廊
⑭ PAVILION 凉亭
⑮ BRIDGE 鹊桥
⑯ BAMBOOS 竹韵
⑰ PAGODA 情人亭（婚庆木亭）
⑱ TRAIL 曲径通曲
⑲ WATERFALL 瀑布
⑳ TEA HOUSE SERVICE ROOM 茶座服务间
㉑ TEA HOUSE 塑月华庭茶座
㉒ STONE BRIDGE 石拱桥
㉓ WATER FOUNTAIN 雪松喷泉
㉔ STONE PATH 石板小径
㉕ CURRENT DECORATIVE CORRIDOR
　现状垂花门
㉖ ENTRANCE PLAZA 入口小广场
㉗ EMERGENCY VEHICLE ENTRANCE
　消防通道入口
㉘ CURRENT WALL 现状围墙
㉙ GRAND LAWN 大草坪
㉚ TRAIL 休闲步道
㉛ EXISTING WATERWAYS
　现状水文
㉜ INDOOR 室内网球场

Top: The detail plan nicely expresses the texture of the materials.
Line + Mark
Below: The abundant colour plays a key role on differentiating the vegetational types, and it should be paid more attention to the brush-work of downward looking above the central lawn.
Line + Mark

north

Sidon Community (South Carolina, US): the picture herein
express the plan contents very clearly and fully, without
any superfluous things, which needs, for the designer,
clear clew and well-knit accomplishment.
Line + Mark

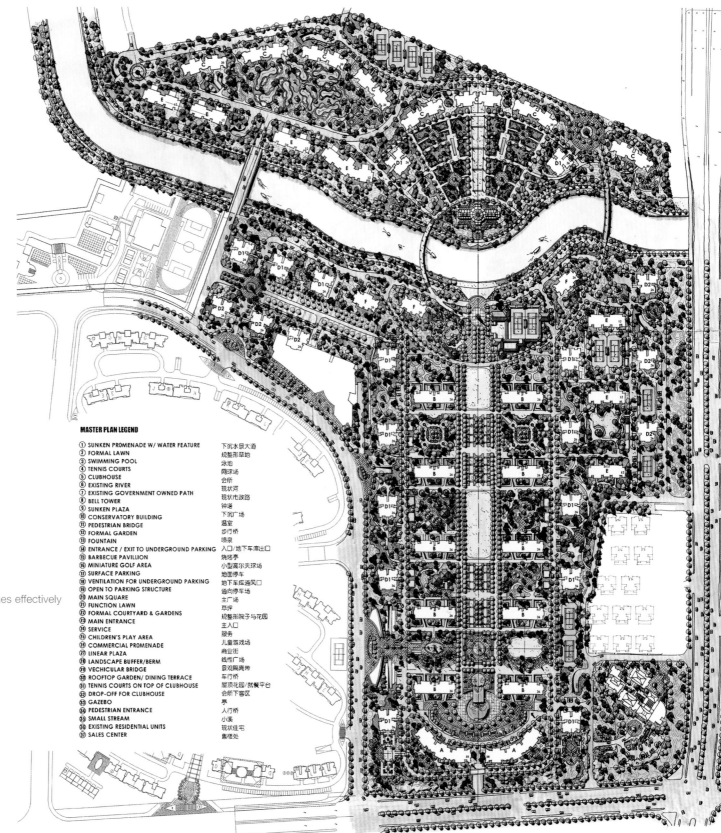

The brushwork of trees in lines effectively
emphasizes the axis.
Line + Mark

MASTER PLAN LEGEND

① SUNKEN PROMENADE W/ WATER FEATURE   下沉水景大道
② FORMAL LAWN   规整形草地
③ SWIMMING POOL   泳池
④ TENNIS COURTS   网球场
⑤ CLUBHOUSE   会所
⑥ EXISTING RIVER   现状河
⑦ EXISTING GOVERNMENT OWNED PATH   现状市政路
⑧ BELL TOWER   钟塔
⑨ SUNKEN PLAZA   下沉广场
⑩ CONSERVATORY BUILDING   温室
⑪ PEDESTRIAN BRIDGE   步行桥
⑫ FORMAL GARDEN   喷泉
⑬ FOUNTAIN   喷泉
⑭ ENTRANCE / EXIT TO UNDERGROUND PARKING   入口/地下车库出口
⑮ BARBECUE PAVILLION   烧烤亭
⑯ MINIATURE GOLF AREA   小型高尔夫球场
⑰ SURFACE PARKING   地面停车
⑱ VENTILATION FOR UNDERGROUND PARKING   地下车库通风口
⑲ OPEN TO PARKING STRUCTURE   通向停车场
⑳ MAIN SQUARE   主广场
㉑ FUNCTION LAWN   草坪
㉒ FORMAL COURTYARD & GARDENS   规整形院子与花园
㉓ MAIN ENTRANCE   主入口
㉔ SERVICE   服务
㉕ CHILDREN'S PLAY AREA   儿童游戏场
㉖ COMMERCIAL PROMENADE   商业街
㉗ LINEAR PLAZA   线性广场
㉘ LANDSCAPE BUFFER/BERM   景观隔离带
㉙ VECHICULAR BRIDGE   车行桥
㉚ ROOFTOP GARDEN/ DINING TERRACE   屋顶花园/就餐平台
㉛ TENNIS COURTS ON TOP OF CLUBHOUSE   会所下客区
㉜ DROP-OFF FOR CLUBHOUSE   会所下客区
㉝ GAZEBO   亭
㉞ PEDESTRIAN ENTRANCE   人行桥
㉟ SMALL STREAM   小溪
㊱ EXISTING RESIDENTIAL UNITS   现状住宅
㊲ SALES CENTER   售楼处

Low Flowering Groundcover

Large Buffer Trees

Low to Medium
Flowering Shrubs

Annuals, Perennials, and
Bulbs Themed Thoughout

Flowering Tree

Mature Canopy Tree

(1) TO CONTEMPORARY GARDEN
(2) TRELLIS
(3) FOUNTAIN
(4) SCULPTURES
(5) SEASONAL FLOWER DISPLAY
(6) TO MARKET PLACE
(7) BOAT DROP-OFF
(8) EUROPEAN GARDEN
(9) TO JAPANESE GARDEN
(10) FORMAL PROMENADE
(11) TO CHRYSANTHEMUM ISLAND

Sculpture Garden

Four Seasons Garden

RESORT POOL AREA

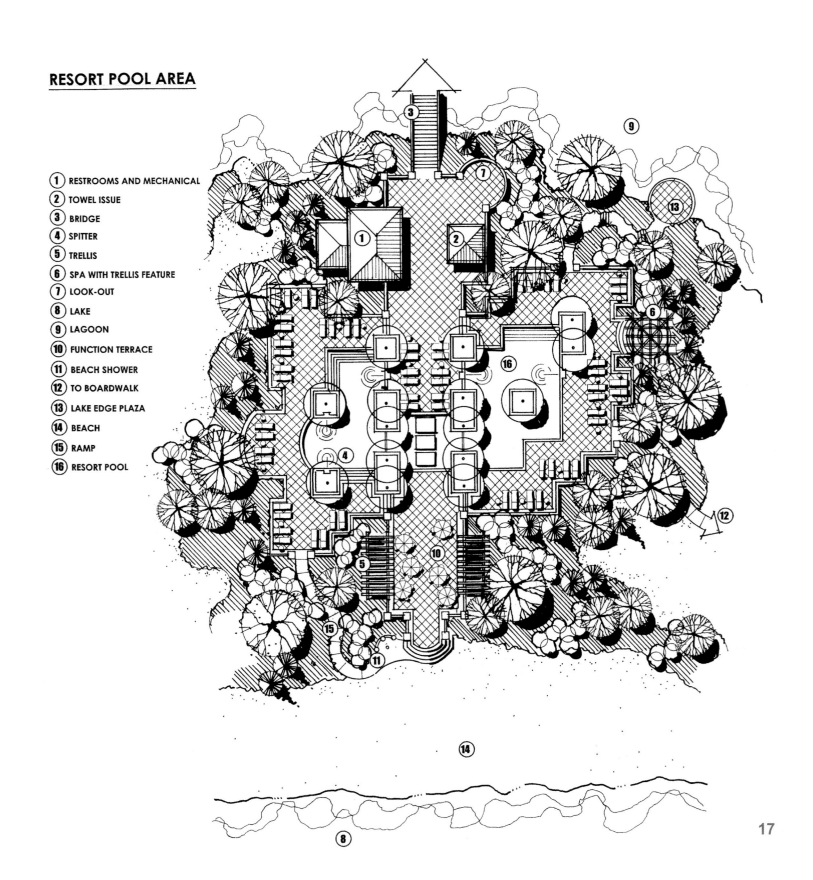

1. RESTROOMS AND MECHANICAL
2. TOWEL ISSUE
3. BRIDGE
4. SPITTER
5. TRELLIS
6. SPA WITH TRELLIS FEATURE
7. LOOK-OUT
8. LAKE
9. LAGOON
10. FUNCTION TERRACE
11. BEACH SHOWER
12. TO BOARDWALK
13. LAKE EDGE PLAZA
14. BEACH
15. RAMP
16. RESORT POOL

17

Large Buffer Trees

Annuals, Perennials, and
Bulbs Themed Thoughout

SECTION 2 ON SHEET T

18

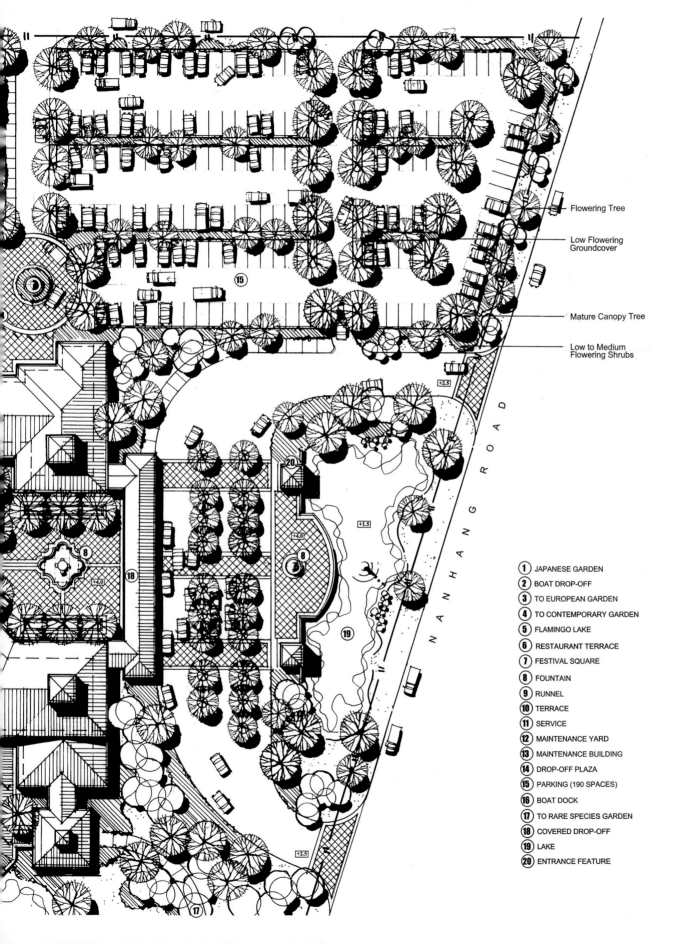

Flowering Tree

Low Flowering
Groundcover

Mature Canopy Tree

Low to Medium
Flowering Shrubs

NANHANG ROAD

① JAPANESE GARDEN
② BOAT DROP-OFF
③ TO EUROPEAN GARDEN
④ TO CONTEMPORARY GARDEN
⑤ FLAMINGO LAKE
⑥ RESTAURANT TERRACE
⑦ FESTIVAL SQUARE
⑧ FOUNTAIN
⑨ RUNNEL
⑩ TERRACE
⑪ SERVICE
⑫ MAINTENANCE YARD
⑬ MAINTENANCE BUILDING
⑭ DROP-OFF PLAZA
⑮ PARKING (190 SPACES)
⑯ BOAT DOCK
⑰ TO RARE SPECIES GARDEN
⑱ COVERED DROP-OFF
⑲ LAKE
⑳ ENTRANCE FEATURE

The structure of the scheme is clear and the expression
herein is mature and perfect.
Ink line + computer treatment

1. LANDSCAPE BUFFER
2. TENNIS COURTS W/ PARKING UNDER
3. PERIMETER SECURITY FENCE
4. GATEHOUSE
5. DECORATIVE ENTRY WALL
6. GOLF CART PATH
7. SPA BUILDING W/ POOL AND GARDEN FEATURE
8. LAKE VIEW UNITS
9. OCEAN VIEW UNITS
10. ENTRY DRIVE
11. FOUNTAIN

12. ENTRANCE TO SERVIC
13. ARRIVAL COURT
14. PORTE COCHERE
15. LAGOON
16. BUNGALOW UNITS
17. LOBBY AREA
18. RESTAURANTS/RETAIN
19. FUNCTION TERRACE
20. STEPS DOWN TO WATE
21. EXISTING LAKE
22. PUBLIC PATH

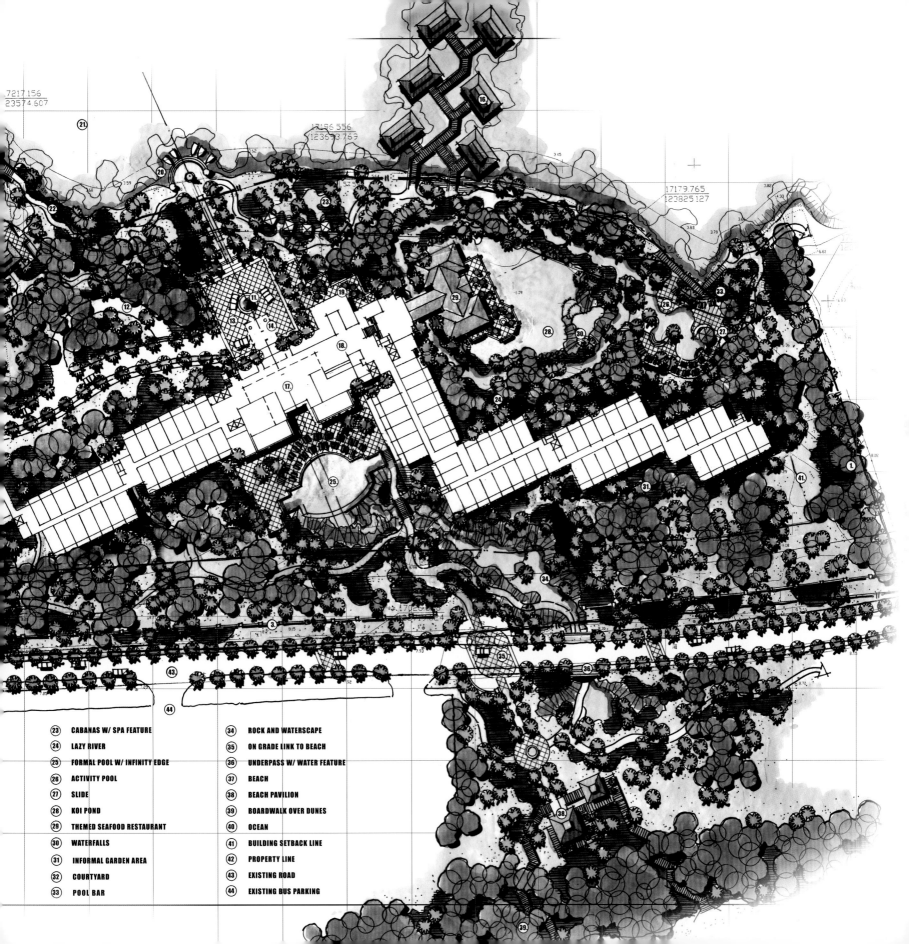

㉓ CABANAS W/ SPA FEATURE	㉞ ROCK AND WATERSCAPE
㉔ LAZY RIVER	㉟ ON GRADE LINK TO BEACH
㉕ FORMAL POOL W/ INFINITY EDGE	㊱ UNDERPASS W/ WATER FEATURE
㉖ ACTIVITY POOL	㊲ BEACH
㉗ SLIDE	㊳ BEACH PAVILION
㉘ KOI POND	㊴ BOARDWALK OVER DUNES
㉙ THEMED SEAFOOD RESTAURANT	㊵ OCEAN
㉚ WATERFALLS	㊶ BUILDING SETBACK LINE
㉛ INFORMAL GARDEN AREA	㊷ PROPERTY LINE
㉜ COURTYARD	㊸ EXISTING ROAD
㉝ POOL BAR	㊹ EXISTING BUS PARKING

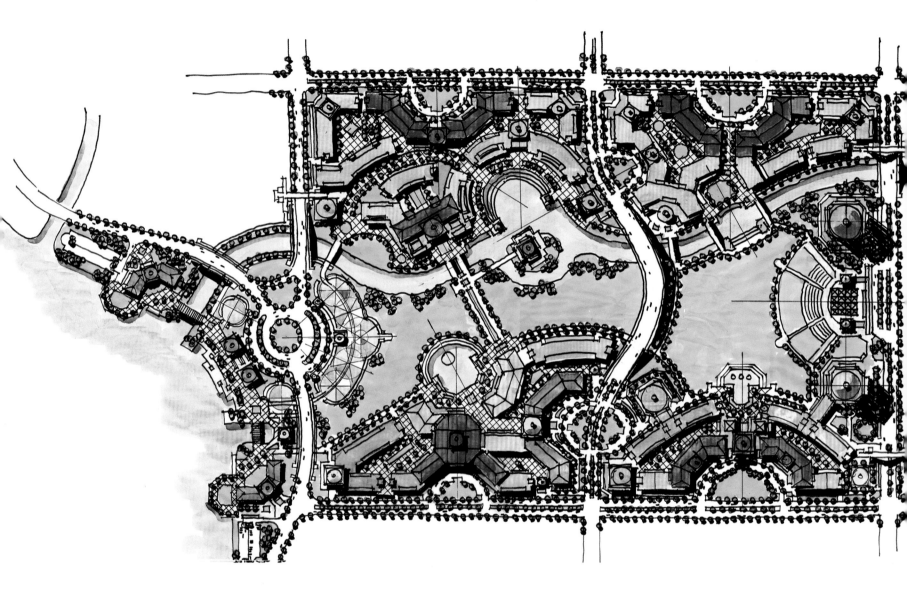

Left: A completely freehand brushwork and, simple and vivid colouring
is of advantage in expressing the conceptional scheme.
Line + Mark
Right: Shanghai Seasons Ecologic Garden. bright colour, forceful
comparison, and appropriate expression.
Line + Mark

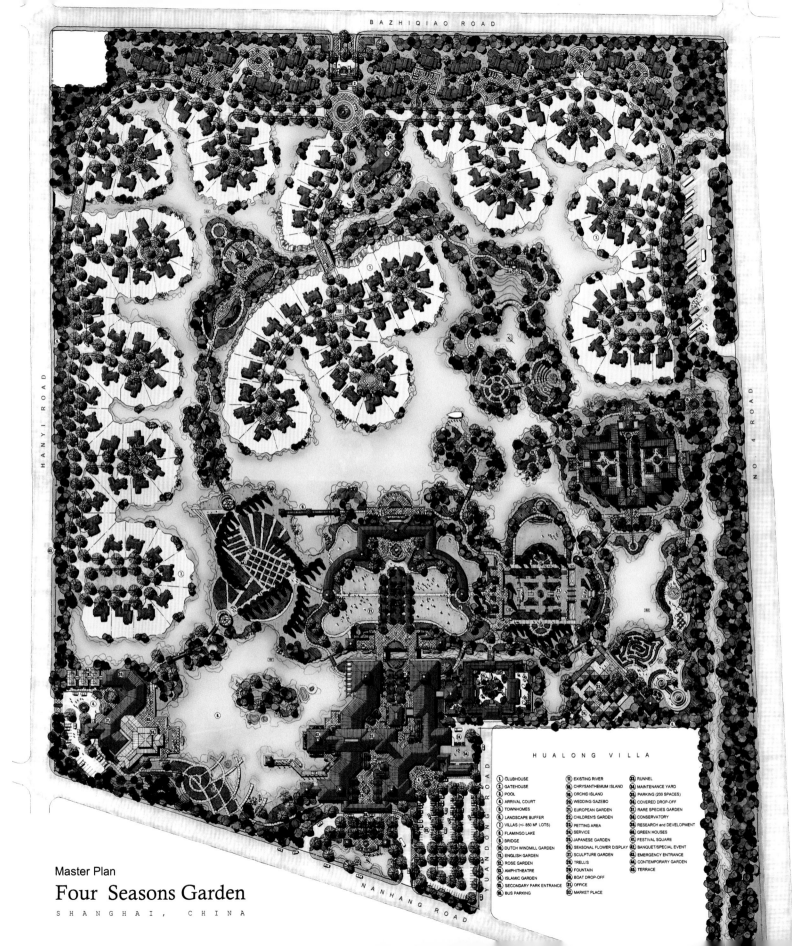

BAZHIQIAO ROAD

HANYI ROAD

NO. 4 ROAD

YUANDONG ROAD

NANHANG ROAD

Master Plan
Four Seasons Garden
SHANGHAI, CHINA

HUALONG VILLA

1. CLUBHOUSE
2. GATEHOUSE
3. POOL
4. ARRIVAL COURT
5. TOWNHOMES
6. LANDSCAPE BUFFER
7. VILLAS (+/- 850 M² LOTS)
8. FLAMINGO LAKE
9. BRIDGE
10. DUTCH WINDMILL GARDEN
11. ENGLISH GARDEN
12. ROSE GARDEN
13. AMPHITHEATRE
14. ISLAMIC GARDEN
15. SECONDARY PARK ENTRANCE
16. BUS PARKING

17. EXISTING RIVER
18. CHRYSANTHEMUM ISLAND
19. ORCHID ISLAND
20. WEDDING GAZEBO
21. EUROPEAN GARDEN
22. CHILDREN'S GARDEN
23. PETTING AREA
24. SERVICE
25. JAPANESE GARDEN
26. SEASONAL FLOWER DISPLAY
27. SCULPTURE GARDEN
28. TRELLIS
29. FOUNTAIN
30. BOAT DROP-OFF
31. OFFICE
32. MARKET PLACE

33. RUNNEL
34. MAINTENANCE YARD
35. PARKING (200 SPACES)
36. COVERED DROP-OFF
37. RARE SPECIES GARDEN
38. CONSERVATORY
39. RESEARCH and DEVELOPMENT
40. GREEN HOUSES
41. FESTIVAL SQUARE
42. BANQUET/SPECIAL EVENT
43. EMERGENCY ENTRANCE
44. CONTEMPORARY GARDEN
45. TERRACE

MASTER PLAN LEGEND 总平面项目索引

1. MARINA 内港
2. FISHERMAN'S WHARF 渔人码头
3. CONFERENCE HOTEL 会议酒店
4. ARRIVAL COURT 入口广场
5. MAIN ENTRANCE 主入口
6. LUXURY HOTEL 主酒店
7. FRESHWATER LAKE 淡水湖
8. BUS STATION 公共汽车站
9. MAIN BOULEVARD 主干道
10. VEHICULAR BRIDGE 车行桥
11. SWIMMING POOL 游泳池
12. LAGOON 泻湖
13. SOUTH CHINA SEA 南海
14. PHASE II GOLF COURSE 二期高尔夫用地
15. SERVICE ROAD 服务环道
16. EXISTING ROAD 现状道路
17. TO ZHUHAI CITY 至珠海市
18. TO FUTURE HIGHWAY 至规划高速公路
19. SURFACE PARKING 地面停车场
20. COURTYARD 庭院
21. TREATMENT POND 海水处理池
22. CANAL 水道
23. THEME PARK ENTRY 主题公园入口
24. ADMINISTRATION ZONE 管理区域
25. HEALTH AND FITNESS CENTER 健身中心
26. PRIVATE VILLAS 别墅酒店
27. THEME PARK ICON 主题公园标志塔
28. FUTURE PHASE FOR THEME PARK 主题公园预留用地
29. BEAUTY SPA 美容中心
30. HOT SPRING CENTER 温泉中心
31. TENNIS COURTS 网球场
32. TERRACE 室外平台
33. WATER FEATURE 水景
34. HONEYMOON SUITES 蜜月套间
35. BOAT DROP-OFF 游艇停靠站
36. PHASE III RESIDENTIAL 三期住宅用地

Guangdong Zhuhai Hot Spring & Restaurant
Holiday Resort
Line + Mark

24

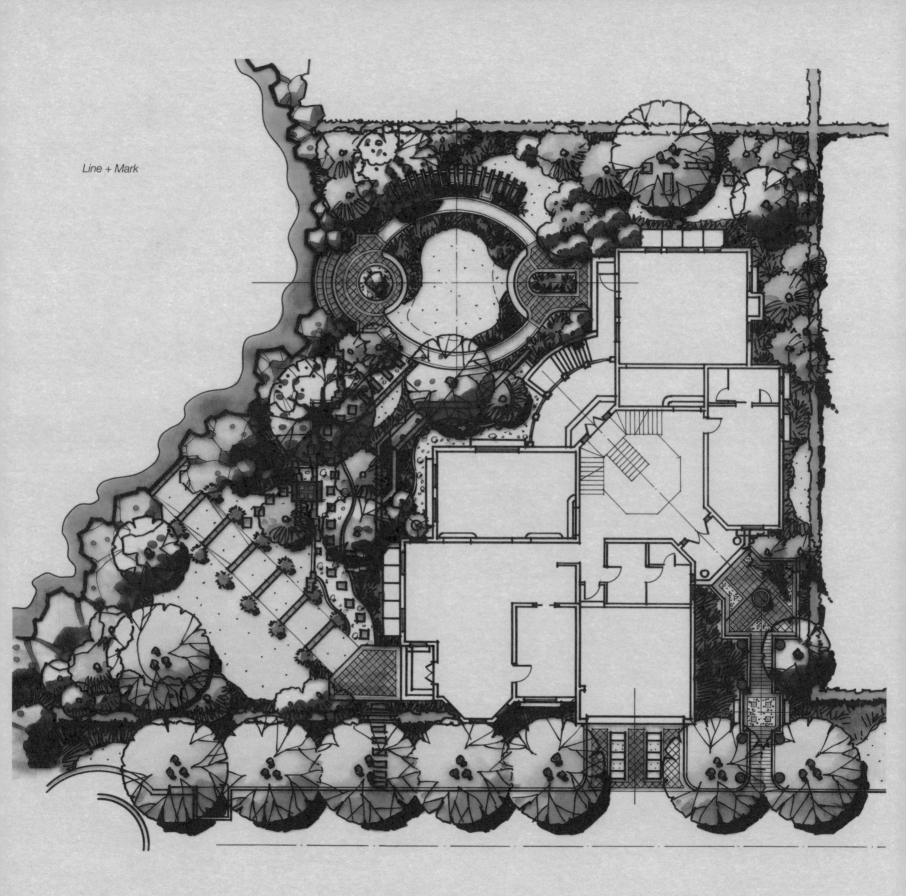

Line + Mark

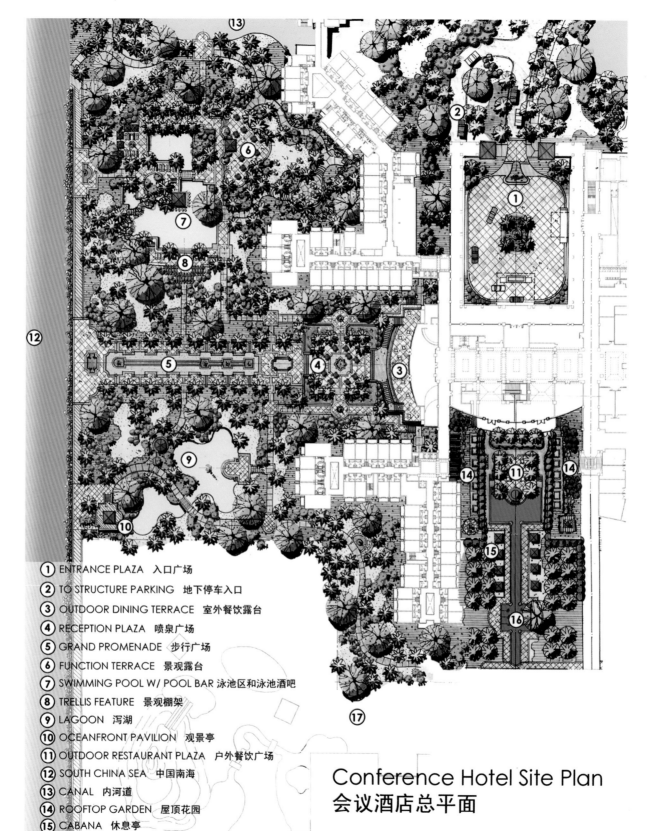

1. ENTRANCE PLAZA 入口广场
2. TO STRUCTURE PARKING 地下停车入口
3. OUTDOOR DINING TERRACE 室外餐饮露台
4. RECEPTION PLAZA 喷泉广场
5. GRAND PROMENADE 步行广场
6. FUNCTION TERRACE 景观露台
7. SWIMMING POOL W/ POOL BAR 泳池区和泳池酒吧
8. TRELLIS FEATURE 景观棚架
9. LAGOON 泻湖
10. OCEANFRONT PAVILION 观景亭
11. OUTDOOR RESTAURANT PLAZA 户外餐饮广场
12. SOUTH CHINA SEA 中国南海
13. CANAL 内河道
14. ROOFTOP GARDEN 屋顶花园
15. CABANA 休息亭
16. RUNNEL FEATURE 景观水渠
17. HOT SPRING CENTER 温泉中心

Conference Hotel Site Plan
会议酒店总平面

0   7.5   15   30m

north

SEPT. 29, 2003
E D S A - ORIENT

27

1 SHANGRI-LA GATEWAY
通往香格里拉
2 PEDESTRIAN BRIDGE
步行桥
3 MAYAN KINGDOM GATEWAY
玛雅区入口
4 WATERWAY
水系
5 RESTAURANT
餐厅
6 SERVICE
服务用地
7 THEMED PAVING MOSAIC
主体特色铺装
8 GIFT SHOP
纪念品商店
9 ENTRY TO GYRO SWING
大摆锤入口区
10 GYRO SWING
大摆锤
11 MINE TRAIN
矿山车
12 SUBMERGED AIRPLANE
淹没的飞机
13 WATERFALL
瀑布
14 SERVICE ROAD
服务流线
15 TRAIN TRACKS
火车轨道
16 TRAIN STATION
火车站
17 RESTROOMS
公共厕所
18 FAST FOOD RESTAURANT
快餐厅
19 DINING TERRACE
室外餐饮区
20 LAGOON
泻湖
21 VIEWING PLAZA
观景广场
22 STAFF/OPERATIONS
后勤区
23 SIDE SHOW ALLEY
摊位游戏
24 ACTIVITY AREA
游戏区
25 TO ATLANTIS PARK
通往亚特兰帝斯
26 DISASTER ZONE
大洪水区
27 UTILITY AND CONTROL ROOM
配电室及控制室
28 MECHANICAL ROOM
变电室

29 BUMPER CARS
碰碰车
30 SECURITY
警卫室
31 TREE HOUSE
树屋
32 ROCK CLIMBING
攀岩
33 BEACH AREA
西班牙海滩
34 PARROT SHOW PLAZA
鹦鹉表演场
35 PARROT CAGE
鹦鹉展示笼
36 EXCAVATION SITE
挖掘现场
37 MAYAN HAT RIDE
玛雅草帽
38 GHOST MONKEY FOREST
鬼猴子森林
39 WATER COMBAT
夺水战斗
40 PERFORMANCE STAGE
表演舞台
41 HAUNTED HOUSE
恐怖听音室
42 WATER GAMES
矿井戏水
43 POTTERY WORKSHOP
陶土作坊
44 FLYING FOX
飞狐雅滑索

28

conceptual site plan

Gentury Overseas Chinese Happy
Valley ecological Theme Park, Beijing
Line + Mark

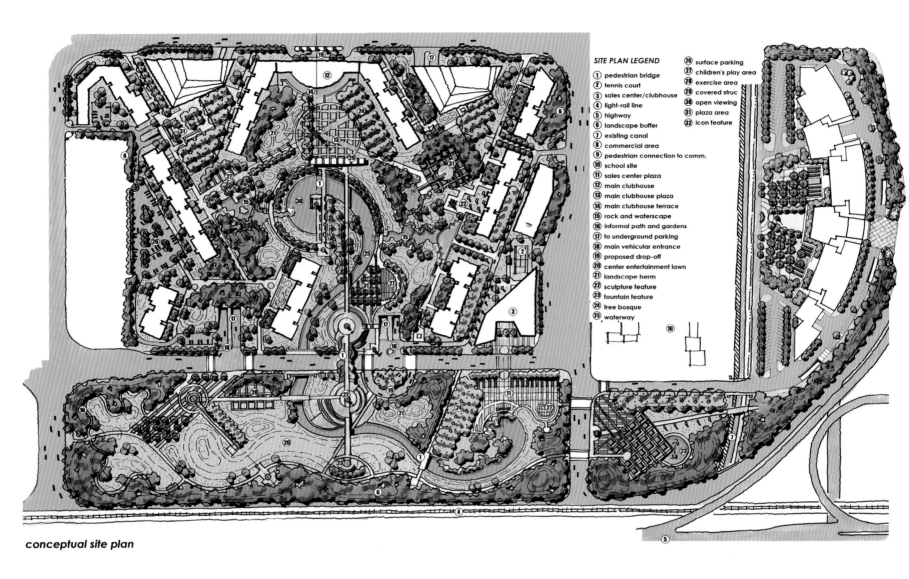

conceptual site plan

SITE PLAN LEGEND

① pedestrian bridge
② tennis court
③ sales center/clubhouse
④ light-rail line
⑤ highway
⑥ landscape buffer
⑦ existing canal
⑧ commercial area
⑨ pedestrian connection to comm.
⑩ school site
⑪ sales center plaza
⑫ main clubhouse
⑬ main clubhouse plaza
⑭ main clubhouse terrace
⑮ rock and waterscape
⑯ informal path and gardens
⑰ to underground parking
⑱ main vehicular entrance
⑲ proposed drop-off
⑳ center entertainment lawn
㉑ landscape berm
㉒ sculpture feature
㉓ fountain feature
㉔ tree bosque
㉕ waterway

㉖ surface parking
㉗ children's play area
㉘ exercise area
㉙ covered struc
㉚ open viewing
㉛ plaza area
㉜ icon feature

Left: Beijing Guanhu International.
Line + Mark
Right: Century Overseas Chinese Happy Valley Theme Park. Virgin Harbor Region, natural brushwork and couspicuous show.
Line + Mark

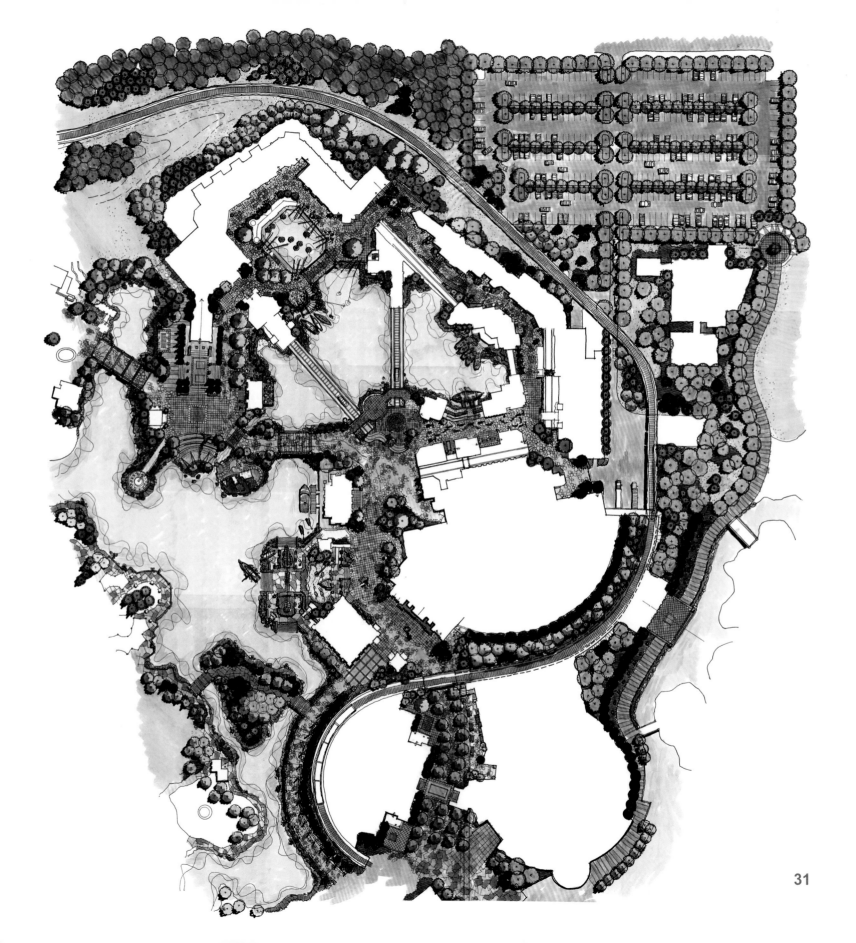

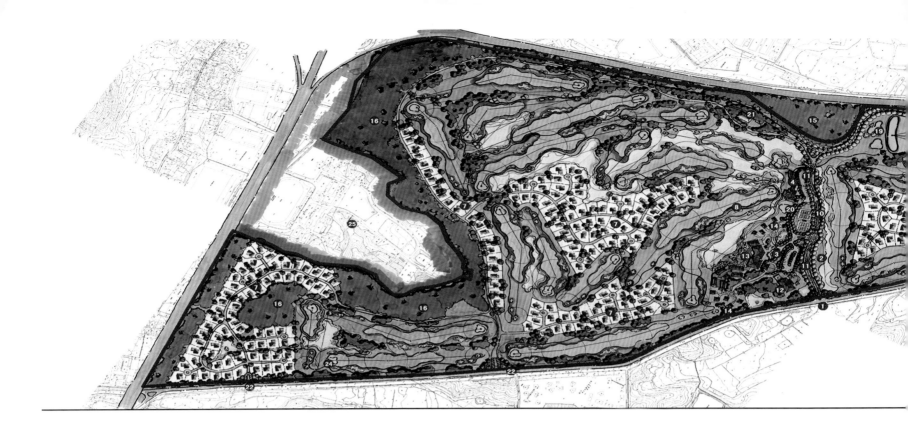

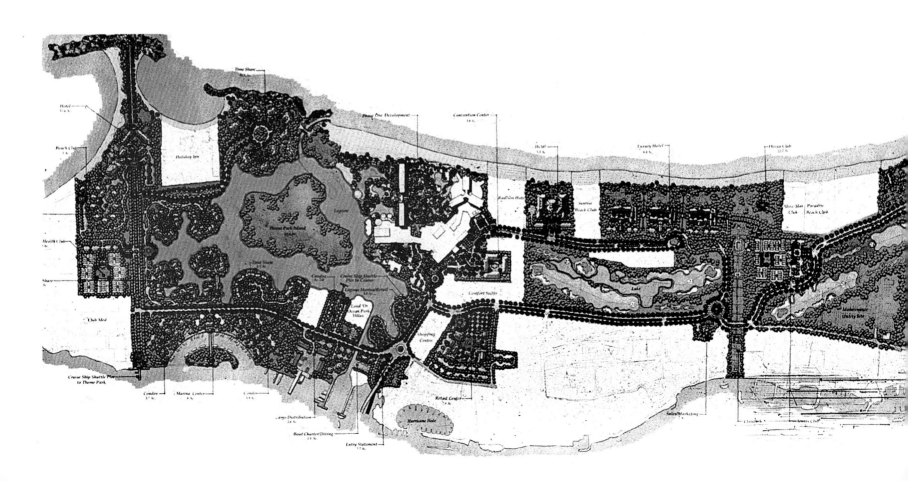

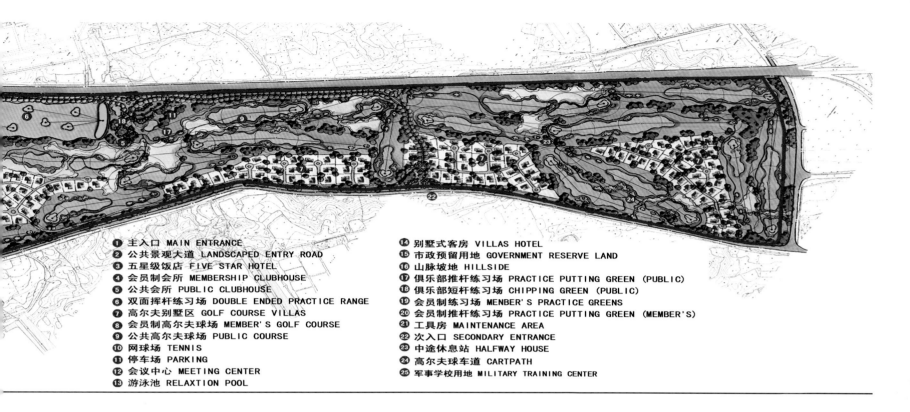

① 主入口 MAIN ENTRANCE			⑭ 别墅式客房 VILLAS HOTEL	
② 公共景观大道 LANDSCAPED ENTRY ROAD			⑮ 市政预留用地 GOVERNMENT RESERVE LAND	
③ 五星级饭店 FIVE STAR HOTEL			⑯ 山脉坡地 HILLSIDE	
④ 会员制会所 MEMBERSHIP CLUBHOUSE			⑰ 俱乐部推杆练习场 PRACTICE PUTTING GREEN (PUBLIC)	
⑤ 公共会所 PUBLIC CLUBHOUSE			⑱ 俱乐部短杆练习场 CHIPPING GREEN (PUBLIC)	
⑥ 双面挥杆练习场 DOUBLE ENDED PRACTICE RANGE			⑲ 会员制练习场 MENBER'S PRACTICE GREENS	
⑦ 高尔夫别墅区 GOLF COURSE VILLAS			⑳ 会员制推杆练习场 PRACTICE PUTTING GREEN (MEMBER'S)	
⑧ 会员制高尔夫球场 MEMBER'S GOLF COURSE			㉑ 工具房 MAINTENANCE AREA	
⑨ 公共高尔夫球场 PUBLIC COURSE			㉒ 次入口 SECONDARY ENTRANCE	
⑩ 网球场 TENNIS			㉓ 中途休息站 HALFWAY HOUSE	
⑪ 停车场 PARKING			㉔ 高尔夫球车道 CARTPATH	
⑫ 会议中心 MEETING CENTER			㉕ 军事学校用地 MILITARY TRAINING CENTER	
⑬ 游泳池 RELAXTION POOL				

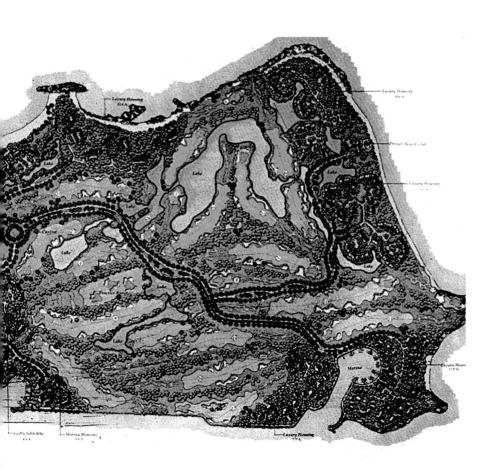

Top: Nanjing Zhongshan International Sports Park
Line + Mark
Below: *Line + Mark*

33

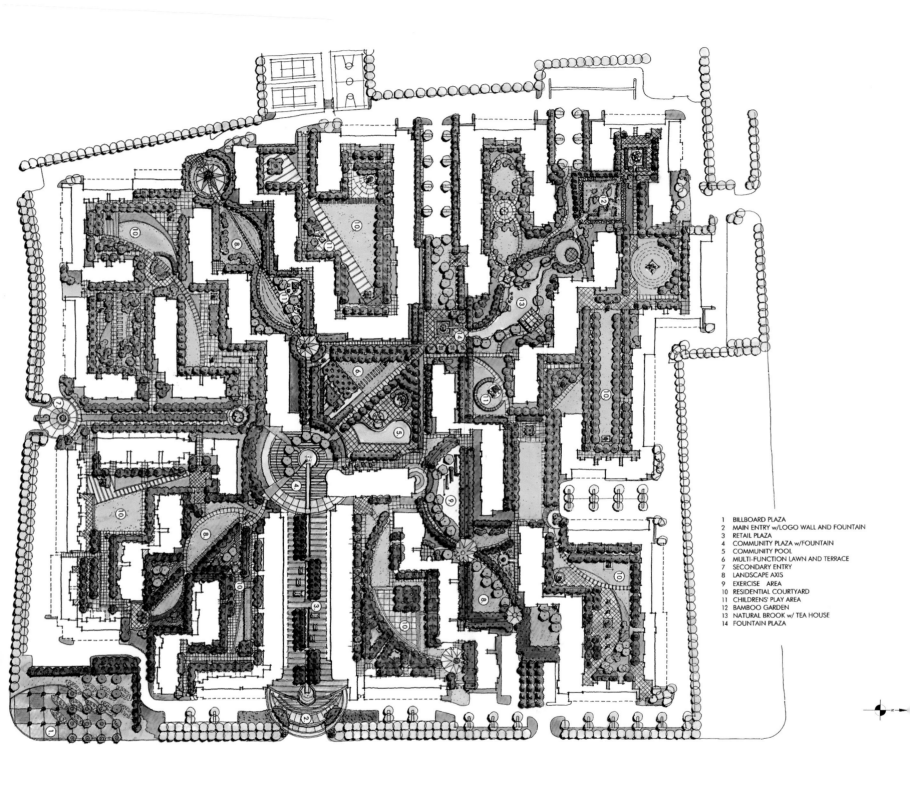

1   BILLBOARD PLAZA
2   MAIN ENTRY w/LOGO WALL AND FOUNTAIN
3   RETAIL PLAZA
4   COMMUNITY PLAZA w/FOUNTAIN
5   COMMUNITY POOL
6   MULTI-FUNCTION LAWN AND TERRACE
7   SECONDARY ENTRY
8   LANDSCAPE AXIS
9   EXERCISE   AREA
10 RESIDENTIAL COURTYARD
11 CHILDRENS' PLAY AREA
12 BAMBOO GARDEN
13 NATURAL BROOK w/ TEA HOUSE
14 FOUNTAIN PLAZA

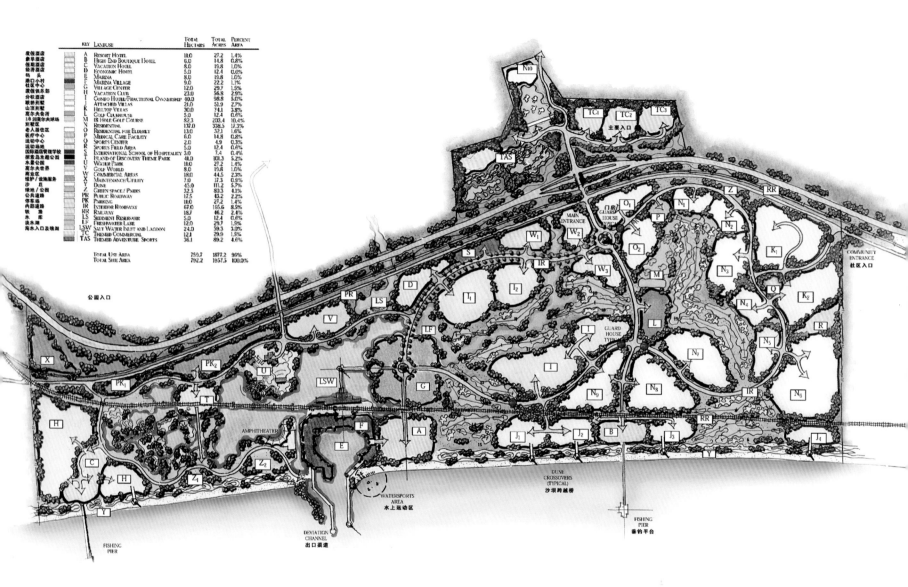

Left: Sichuan Chengdu Borui City Garden.
Line + Mark
Right: Hainan Sanya Hongtang Bay. The brushwork herein is recapitulatory, and suitable for conceptional scheme phase of a large-scale project.
Line + Mark

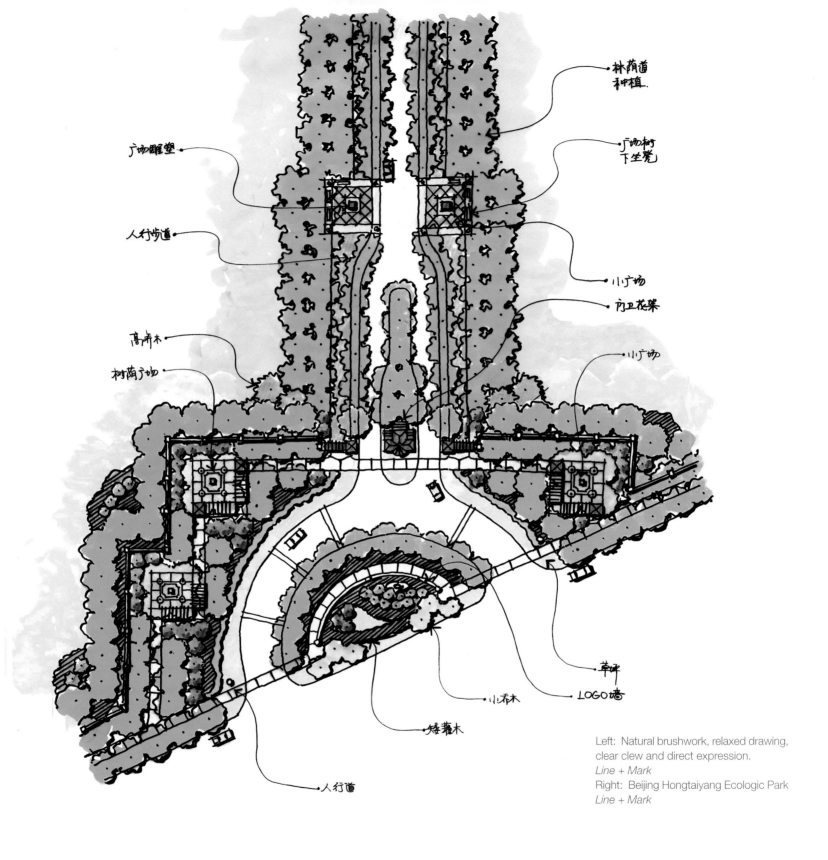

林荫道
种植.

广场雕塑

广场树
下坐凳

人行步道

小广场

内卫花架

高乔木

树荫广场

小广场

草坪

小乔木

LOGO墙

矮灌木

人行道

Left: Natural brushwork, relaxed drawing,
clear clew and direct expression.
Line + Mark
Right: Beijing Hongtaiyang Ecologic Park
Line + Mark

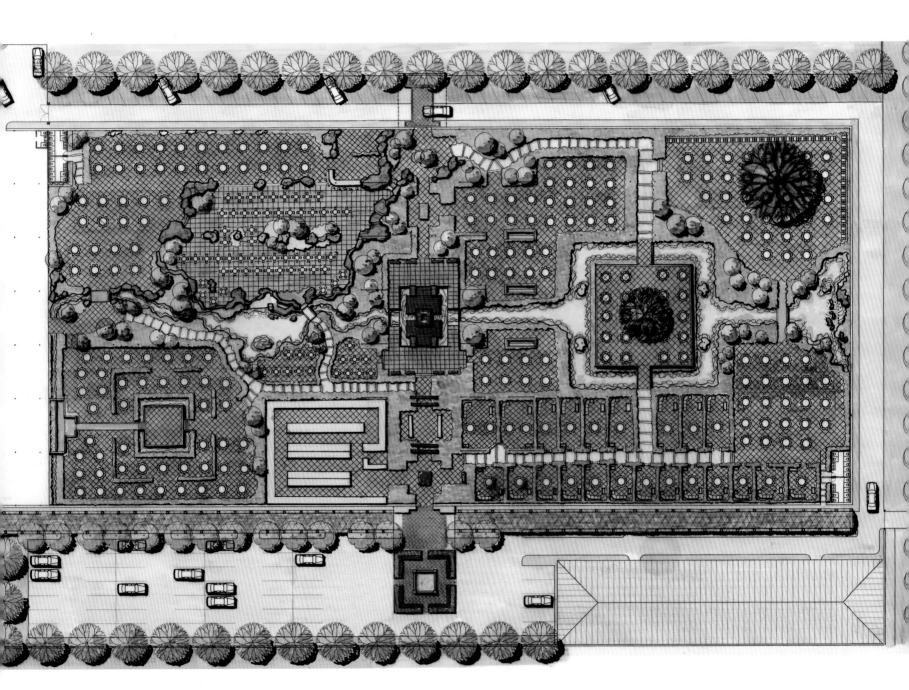

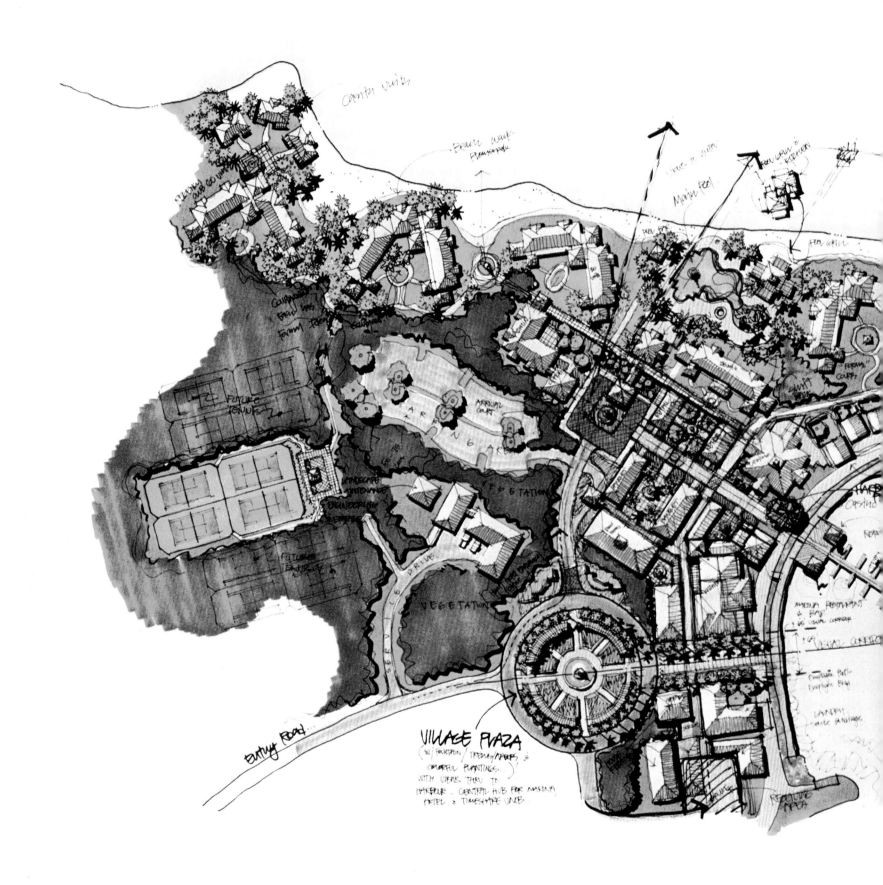

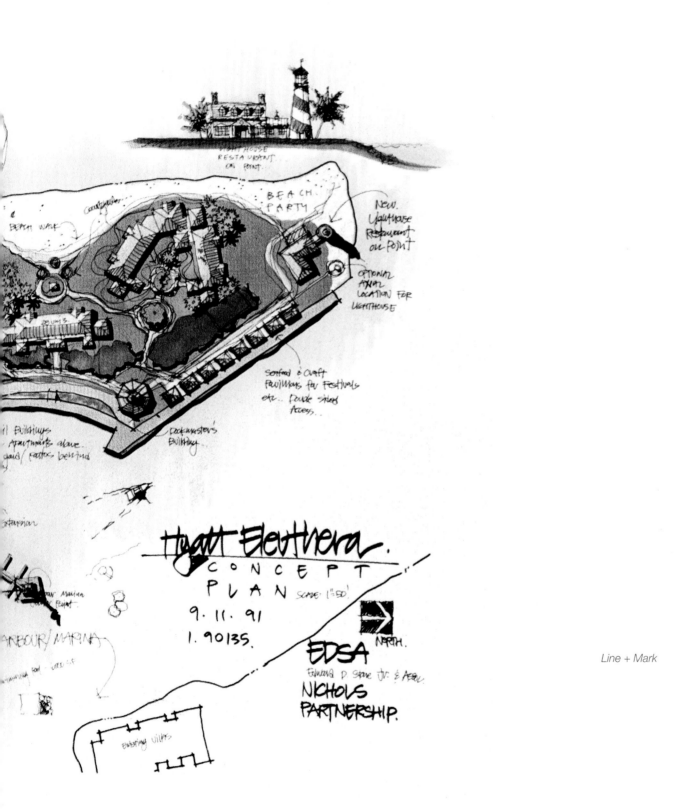

Lighthouse
Restaurant
on Point

BEACH
PARTY

New.
Lighthouse
Restaurant
on Point

BEACH WALK

Optional
Axial
Location for
Lighthouse

DRUMS

Seafood & Craft
Pavilions for Festivals
etc. Double Sided
Access.

Buildings
Apartments above
guad / patios behind

Dockmaster's
Building

catamaran

Marina
Point

HARBOUR / MARINA

swimming pool - cold soft

Hyatt Eleuthera.
C O N C E P T
P L A N SCALE 1"=50'
9 . 11 . 91
1 . 90135.

NORTH.

EDSA
Edward D. Stone Jr. & Assoc.
NICHOLS
PARTNERSHIP.

Existing Villas

Line + Mark

39

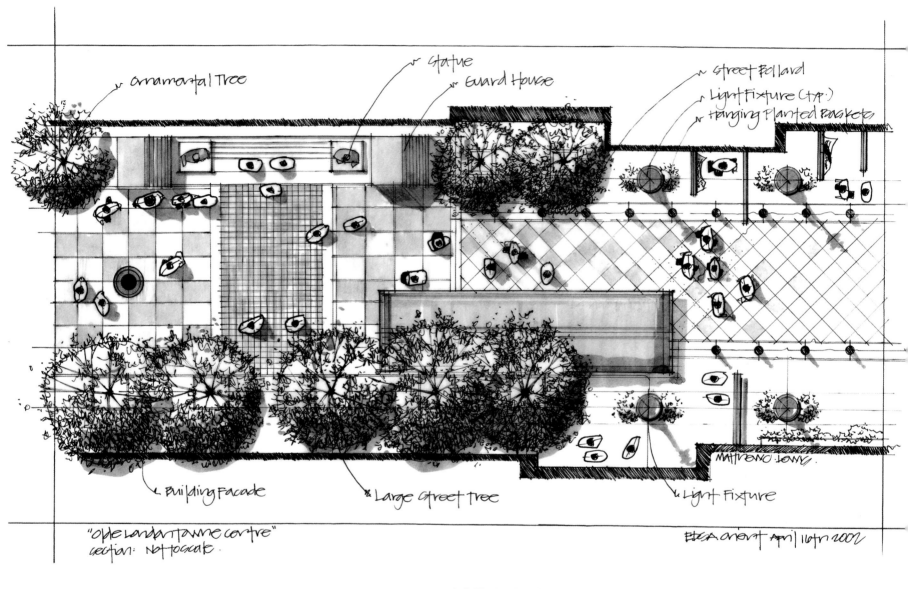

Ornamental Tree

Statue

Guard House

Street Bollard

Light Fixture (TP.)

Hanging Planted Baskets

Building Facade

Large Street Tree

Light Fixture

"Olde London Towne Centre"
Section: Not to scale.

EDSA Orient April 16th 2002

Left: The brushwork of the trees is very living and has a
vivid comparison to the lines. That of human is also
interesting, and provides a scale sensation.
Line + Mark
Right: Line + Mark

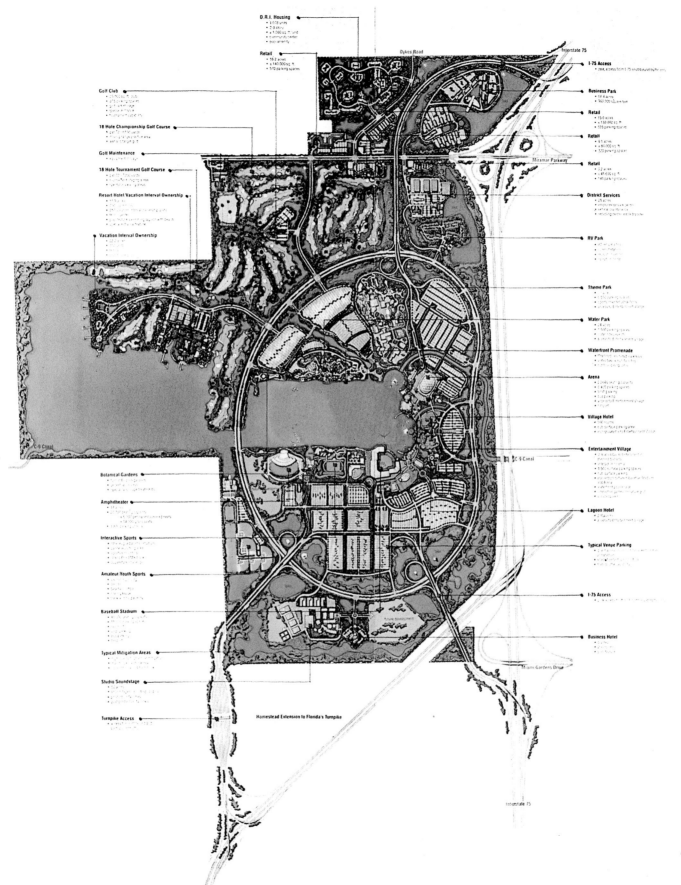

D.R.I. Housing

Retail

Golf Club

18 Hole Championship Golf Course

Golf Maintenance

18 Hole Tournament Golf Course

Resort Hotel Vacation Interval Ownership

Vacation Interval Ownership

Botanical Gardens

Amphitheater

Interactive Sports

Amateur/Youth Sports

Baseball Stadium

Typical Mitigation Areas

Studio Soundstage

Turnpike Access

I-75 Access

Business Park

Retail

Retail

Retail

District Services

RV Park

Theme Park

Water Park

Waterfront Promenade

Arena

Village Hotel

Entertainment Village

Lagoon Hotel

Typical Venue Parking

I-75 Access

Business Hotel

Dykes Road

Interstate 75

Miramar Parkway

C-9 Canal

C-8 Canal

Homestead Extension to Florida's Turnpike

Miami Gardens Drive

Interstate 75

41

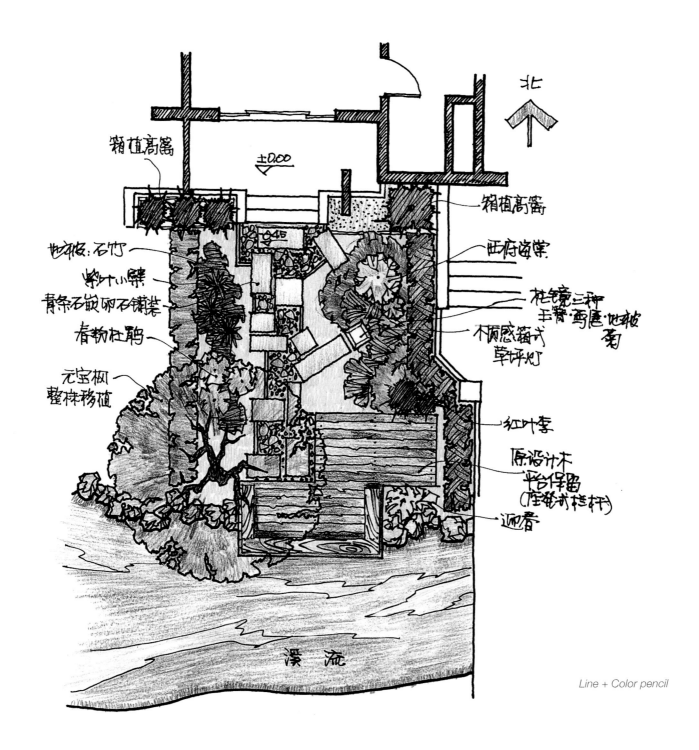

箱植高篱

箱植高篱

地被：石竹

西府海棠

紫叶小檗

青条石嵌卵石铺装

花镜宽三种
玉簪·鸢尾·地被菊

春物杜鹃

木质感箱式
草坪灯

元宝枫
整株移植

红叶李

原设计木
平台保留
(控钢式栏杆)

迎春

±0.00

0.45

北

漠流

Line + Color pencil

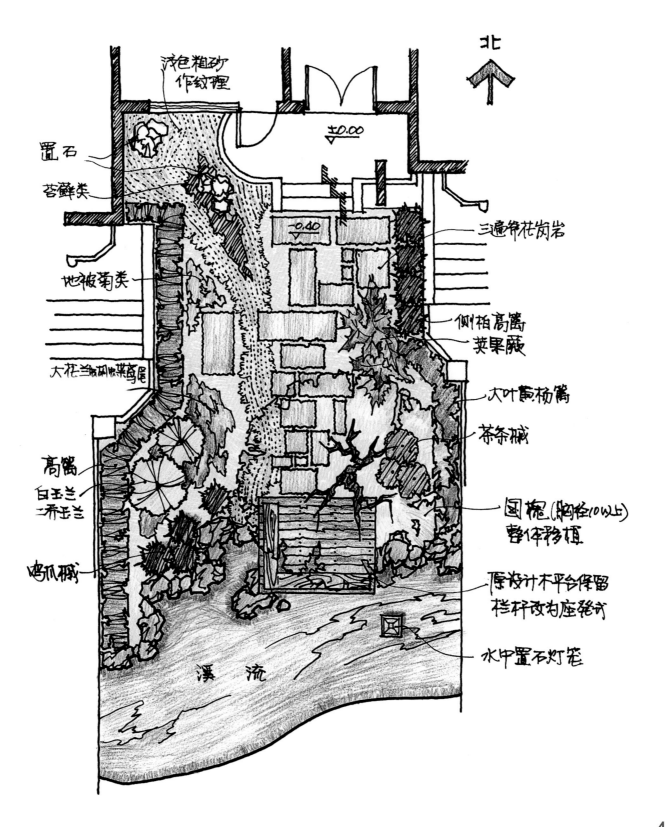

北

浅色粗砂作纹理

置石

苔藓类

地被菊类

大花萱草细叶鸢尾

高篱
白玉兰
二乔玉兰

鸡爪槭

溪　　流

±0.00

-0.40

三遍待花岗岩

侧柏高篱
荚果蕨

大叶黄杨篱

茶条槭

国槐(胸径10以上)整体移植

原设计木平台保留
栏杆改为座凳式

水中置石灯笼

43

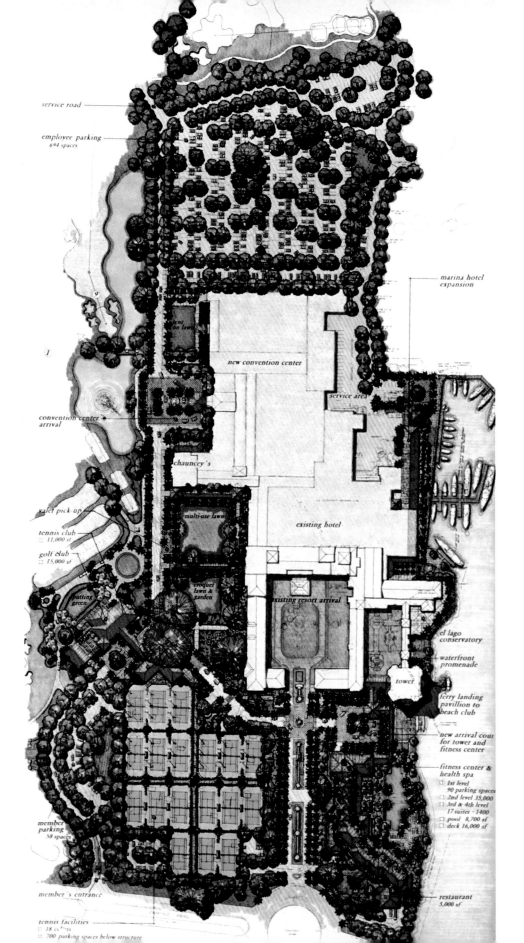

service road

employee parking
694 spaces

marina hotel
expansion

new convention center

service area

convention center
arrival

chauncey's

valet pick-up

multi-use lawn

existing hotel

tennis club
☐ 11,000 sf

golf club
☐ 15,000 sf

croquet
lawn &
garden

el lago
conservatory

existing resort arrival

putting
green

waterfront
promenade

tower

ferry landing
pavillion to
beach club

new arrival court
for tower and
fitness center

fitness center &
health spa
☐ 1st level
90 parking spaces
☐ 2nd level 33,000
☐ 3rd & 4th level
17 suites - 1400
☐ pool 8,700 sf
☐ deck 16,000 sf

member
parking
58 spaces

member's entrance

restaurant
5,000 sf

tennis facilities
☐ 18 courts
☐ 700 parking spaces below structure

44

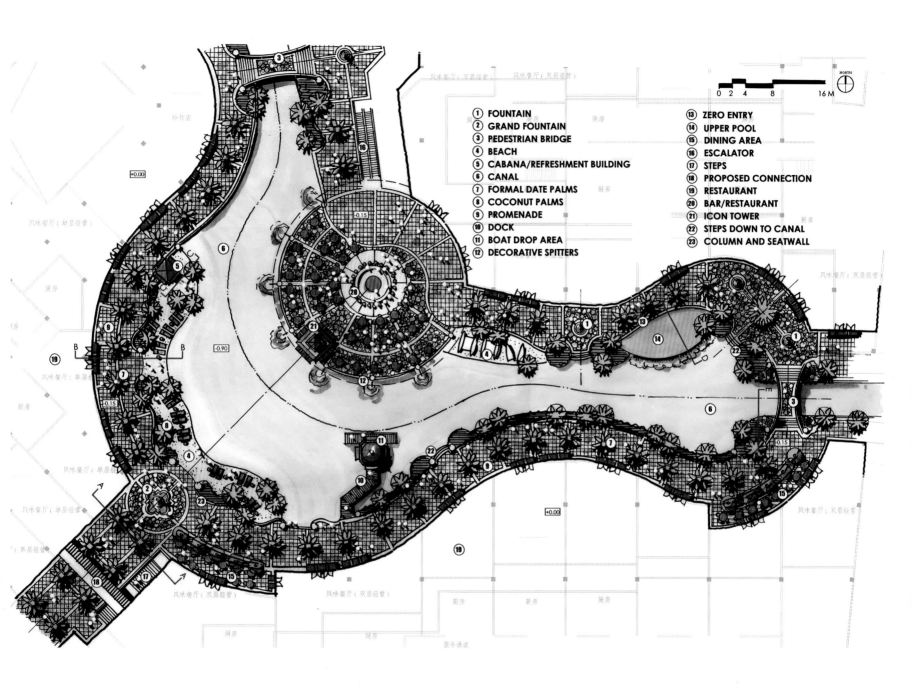

①	FOUNTAIN		⑬	ZERO ENTRY
②	GRAND FOUNTAIN		⑭	UPPER POOL
③	PEDESTRIAN BRIDGE		⑮	DINING AREA
④	BEACH		⑯	ESCALATOR
⑤	CABANA/REFRESHMENT BUILDING		⑰	STEPS
⑥	CANAL		⑱	PROPOSED CONNECTION
⑦	FORMAL DATE PALMS		⑲	RESTAURANT
⑧	COCONUT PALMS		⑳	BAR/RESTAURANT
⑨	PROMENADE		㉑	ICON TOWER
⑩	DOCK		㉒	STEPS DOWN TO CANAL
⑪	BOAT DROP AREA		㉓	COLUMN AND SEATWALL
⑫	DECORATIVE SPITTERS			

Left: *Line + Mark*
Right: Caribbean Counteryard
Line + Mark

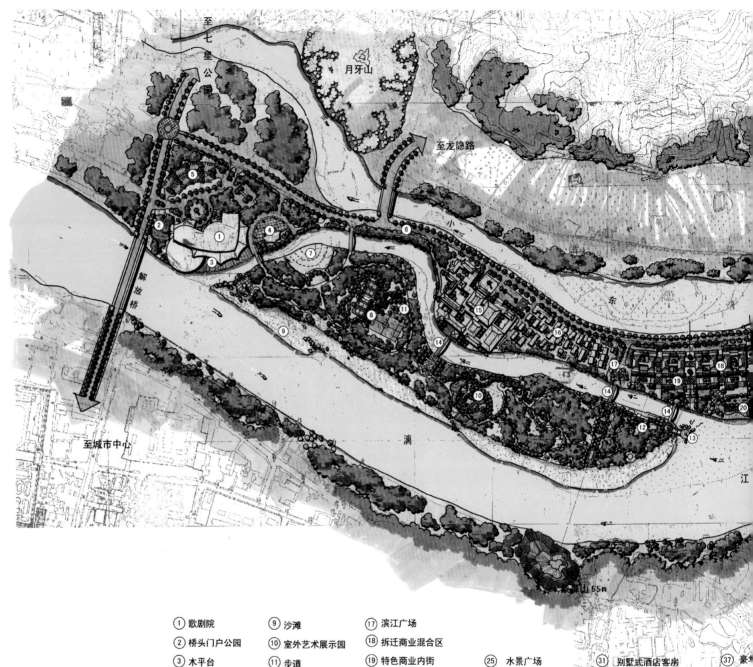

① 歌剧院　　　⑨ 沙滩　　　　　⑰ 滨江广场

② 桥头门户公园　⑩ 室外艺术展示园　⑱ 拆迁商业混合区

③ 木平台　　　　⑪ 步道　　　　　⑲ 特色商业内街　　㉕ 水景广场　　　㉛ 别墅式酒店客房　　㊲ 豪

④ 室外音乐广场　⑫ 服务设施　　　⑳ 滨江休闲商业街　㉖ 酒店入口水景　㉜ 集中拆迁居住区　　㊳ 滨

⑤ 停车场　　　　⑬ 码头　　　　　㉑ 桥头公园　　　　㉗ 酒店大堂　　　㉝ 中心花园　　　　　㊴ 景

⑥ 穿山路　　　　⑭ 景观桥　　　　㉒ 国际休闲商业公园　㉘ 室外晚餐平台　㉞ 别墅区主入口　　㊵ 塔

⑦ 缓坡草坪　　　⑮ 桂山大酒店　　㉓ 室外广场　　　　㉙ 隐边泳池　　　㉟ 会所　　　　　　㊶ 别

⑧ 体育中心　　　⑯ 皆州苑　　　　㉔ 滨江广场　　　　㉚ 酒店客房　　　㊱ 江景豪宅　　　　㊷ 穿

Guilin Lijiang Under-the-Sky
Line + Mark

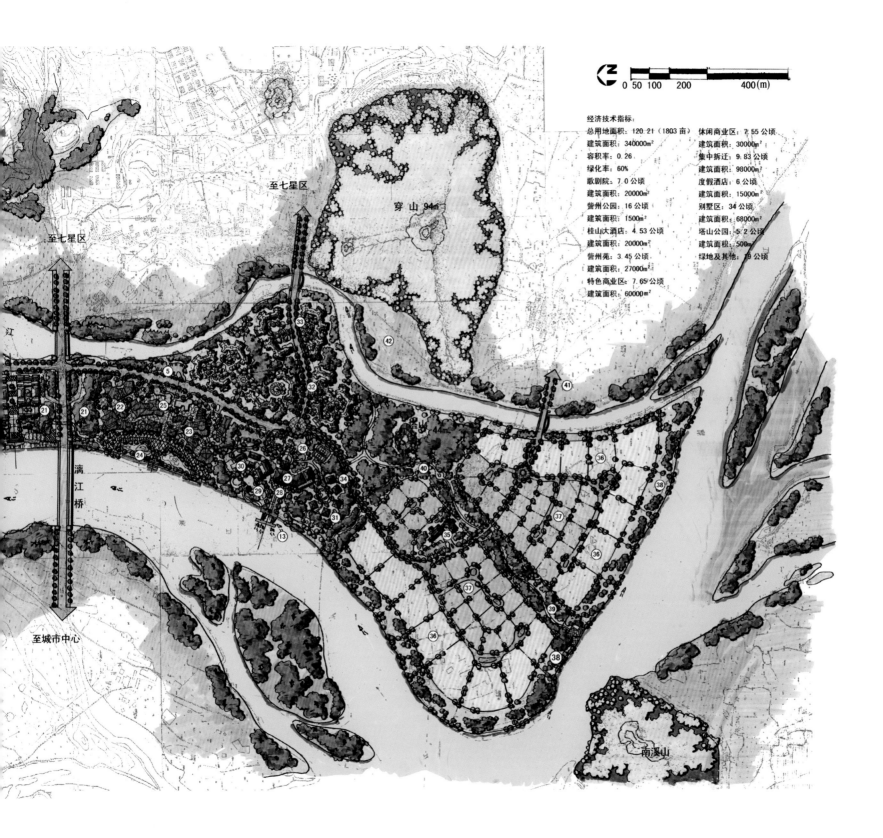

至七星区

穿山 94m

至七星区

至城市中心

漓江桥

江

33

42

5

32

41

21 21 22 25

23

26

40

36

30

24

27 34

38

29 28

31 37

13

35

36

36

39

38

37

南溪山

经济技术指标:

总用地面积: 120.21 (1803 亩)　　　　休闲商业区: 7.55 公顷
建筑面积: 340000m²　　　　　　　　建筑面积: 30000m²
容积率: 0.26　　　　　　　　　　　集中拆迁: 9.83 公顷
绿化率: 60%　　　　　　　　　　　建筑面积: 98000m²
歌剧院: 7.0 公顷　　　　　　　　　度假酒店: 6 公顷
建筑面积: 20000m²　　　　　　　　建筑面积: 15000m²
訾州公园: 16 公顷　　　　　　　　别墅区: 34 公顷
建筑面积: 1500m²　　　　　　　　　建筑面积: 68000m²
桂山大酒店: 4.53 公顷　　　　　　塔山公园: 5.2 公顷
建筑面积: 20000m²　　　　　　　　建筑面积: 500m²
訾州苑: 3.45 公顷　　　　　　　　绿地及其他: 19 公顷
建筑面积: 27000m²
特色商业区: 7.65 公顷
建筑面积: 60000m²

0 50 100 200 400(m)

EDSA (Asian)

Facade View

Atlantis : The lines extend gracefully and moderately, and magnificently show a leisurable atmosphere.
Line + Mark

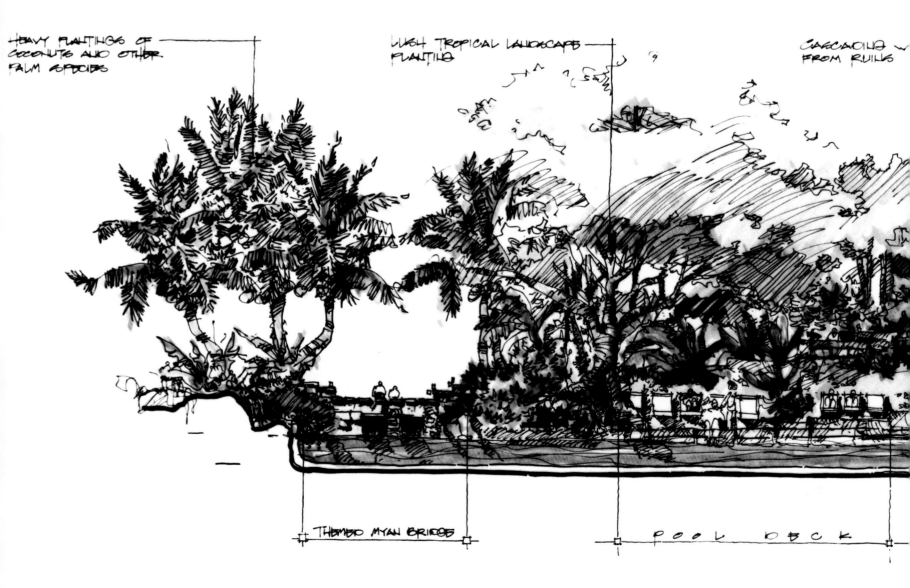

HEAVY PLANTINGS OF COCONUTS AND OTHER PALM SPECIES

LUSH TROPICAL LANDSCAPE PLANTING

CASCADING FROM RUINS

THEMED MYAN BRIDGE

POOL DECK

AQUADUCT / RIVER
RIDE

LUSH TROPICAL LANDSCAPE
PLANTINGS

RIVER RIDE

POOL GROTTO AREA

51

The elegantly distributing of the lines, together with the colors,
nicely express the relationship between space and site.
Line + Mark

CHANGING FACILITY ROOM.

'TEMPLE OF WATER GOD'   PLUNGE POOL   U P P E R   T E R R A C E

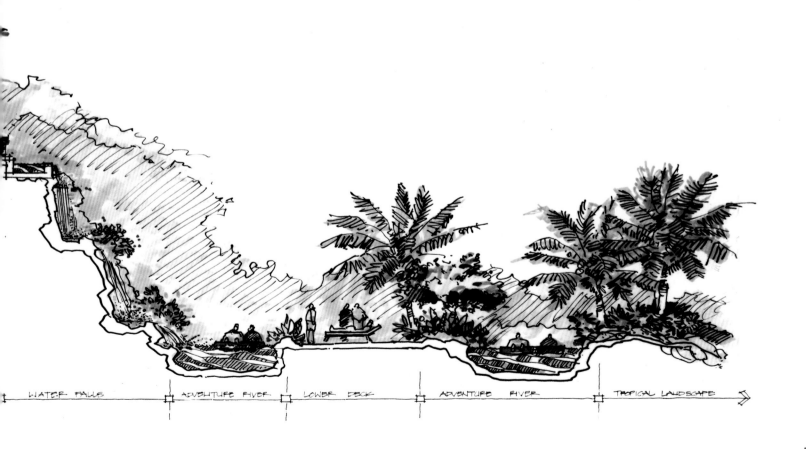

WATER FALLS | ADVENTURE RIVER | LOWER DECK | ADVENTURE RIVER | TROPICAL LANDSCAPE

WATER TUBE/
THROUGH AQUA

E D S A
EDWARD D. STONE JR. and ASSOC.
LANDSCAPE ARCHITECTS and LANDPLANNERS
JANUARY 10, 1996

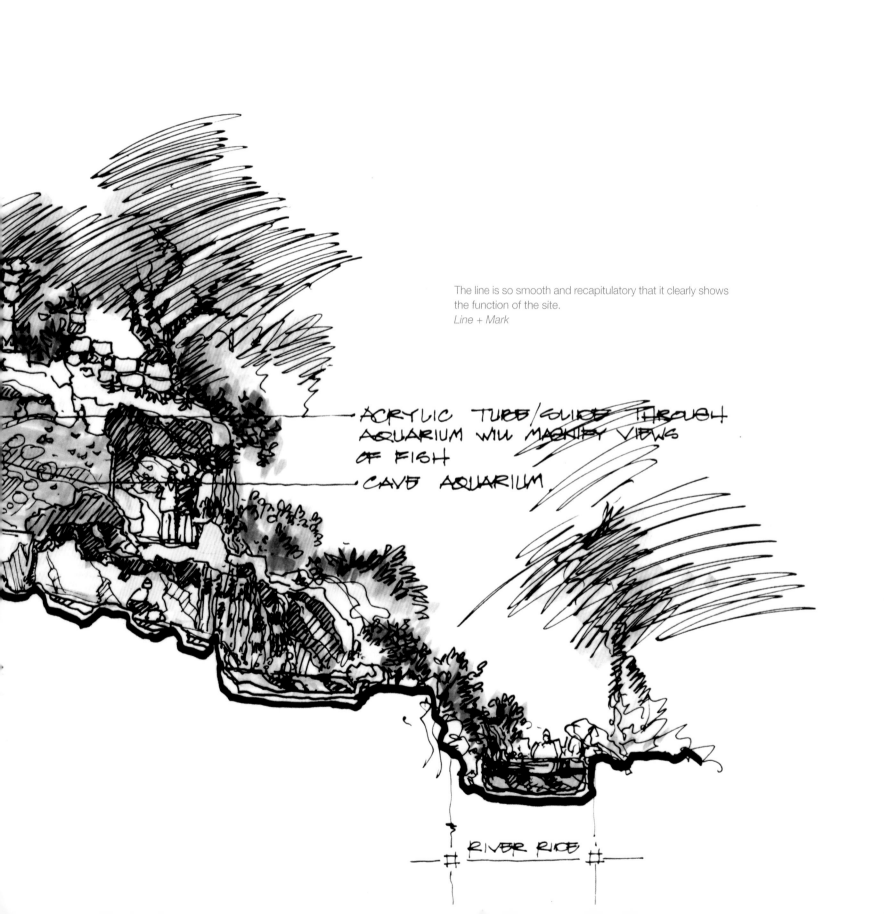

The line is so smooth and recapitulatory that it clearly shows the function of the site.
Line + Mark

ACRYLIC TUBE/SLIDE THROUGH
AQUARIUM WILL MAGNIFY VIEWS
OF FISH

CAVE AQUARIUM

RIVER RIDE

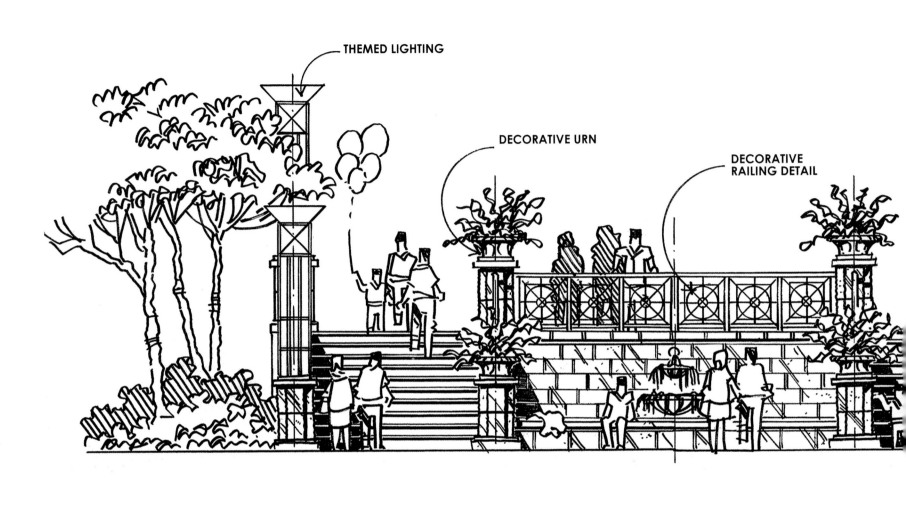

THEMED LIGHTING

DECORATIVE URN

DECORATIVE
RAILING DETAIL

34.70

33.50

Top: The left picture highly makes account
of treatment of edges, or in other word,
interfaces.
Below: *Line*

10 FT. CT. DATE PALM.

TOPIARY

SAGO PALMS.

SIM. CONCRETE LOGS

GRAVELS

BRICK EDGING

LARGE ARTIFICIAL BOULDERS.

58

SOLITAIRE PALMS.

PYGMY DATE PALMS.

QIU RESIDENCE ※ DAVID CHEN 1997.

Treatment of edges, i.e. of interfaces, is a very important part of landscape design. This picture is superior in this aspect. The whole picture is dreamy and serene, and shows the contents herein fully and accurately. The simple and natural brush-work herein delivers a large number of information.
Line + Mark

Top: Club. To mainly show the building, the landscape plants should be concise and clear.
Line + Mark
Below : In site designing, plants have a function of dividing the space.
Line + Mark + Color pencil

SECTION A.A. ENTRANCE "GATES" + SUNKEN COURTYARD.
SECTION.

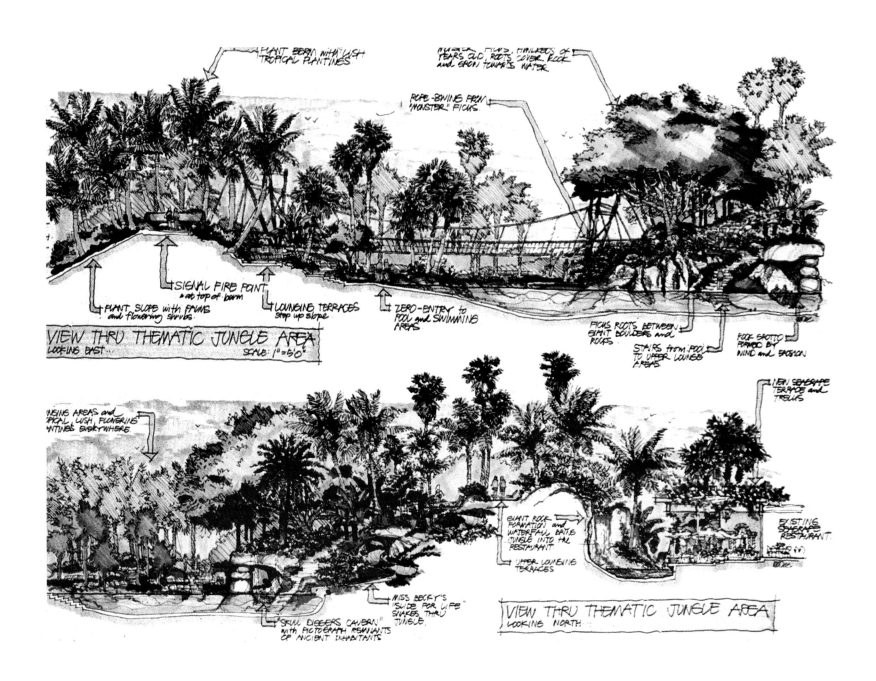

PLANT BERM WITH LUSH TROPICAL PLANTINGS

MONSTER FICUS, HUNDREDS OF YEARS OLD, ROOTS COVER ROCK AND GROW TOWARDS WATER

ROPE-SWING FROM "MONSTER" FICUS

PLANT SLOPE WITH PALMS and flowering shrubs

SIGNAL FIRE POINT - at top of berm

LOUNGING TERRACES step up slope

ZERO-ENTRY to POOL and SWIMMING AREAS

FICUS ROOTS BETWEEN GIANT BOULDERS and ROCKS

STAIRS FROM POOL TO UPPER LOUNGE AREAS

ROCK GROTTO FORMED BY WIND and EROSION

VIEW THRU THEMATIC JUNGLE AREA
LOOKING EAST..   SCALE 1"=5'0"

LOUNGING AREAS and TROPICAL, LUSH, FLOWERING PLANTINGS EVERYWHERE.

NEW SHADE TERRACE and TRELLIS

GIANT ROCK FORMATION and WATERFALL BRING JUNGLE INTO THE RESTAURANT

EXISTING SHADE/ROPE RESTAURANT.

UPPER LOUNGING TERRACES

"SKULL DIGGERS CAVERN" WITH PICTOGRAPH REMNANTS OF ANCIENT INHABITANTS

MISS BECKY'S "SNAKE FOR LIFE" SNAKES THRU JUNGLE

VIEW THRU THEMATIC JUNGLE AREA
LOOKING NORTH

Line + Mark

Line + Mark

Top: Brine pan. The pure colors herein shows a stratified waterfront commercial space.
Line + Mark

65

Left: *Line + Mark*
Top right: *Line*
Lower: Brushwork of the view of theme parks.
Line + Mark

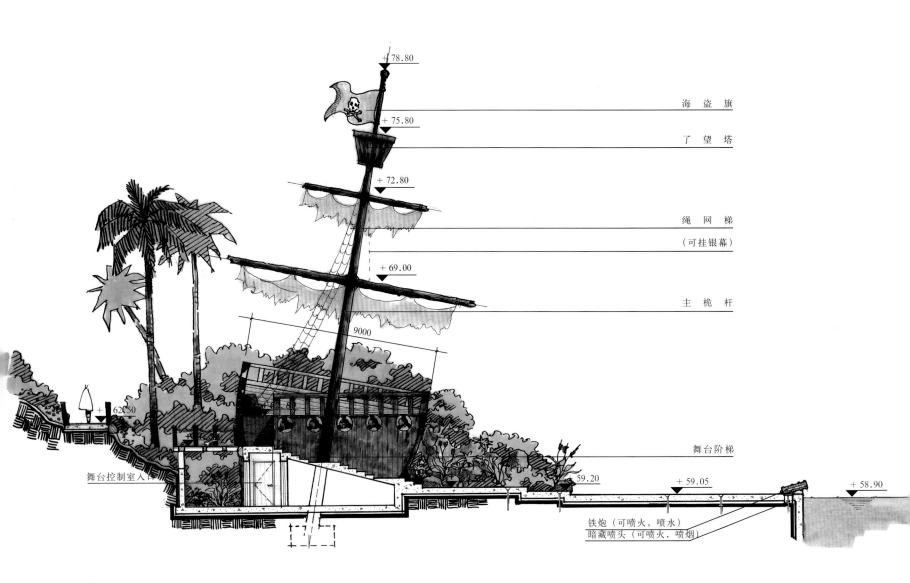

+ 78.80

海 盗 旗

+ 75.80

了 望 塔

+ 72.80

绳 网 梯

（可挂银幕）

+ 69.00

主 桅 杆

9000

+ 62.50

舞台阶梯

舞台控制室入口

59.20

+ 59.05

+ 58.90

铁炮（可喷火，喷水）

暗藏喷头（可喷火，喷烟）

66

HEYUAN PIRATE SHIP & POOL
PERFORMANCE AREA   1:100

TO
KIDDIE POOLS   GARDEN   CONTROLLED ACCESS BRIDGE   PERFORMANCE STAGE 20m   PIRATE SHIP STAGE/DISCO   CASCADING WATERFALL
                              10m   AND PERFORMANCE POOL 32m   18m

67

DEPOT EXIT

MINOTAUR 4.7
W/ BASE

Left: *Line*
Right: *Line + Mark*

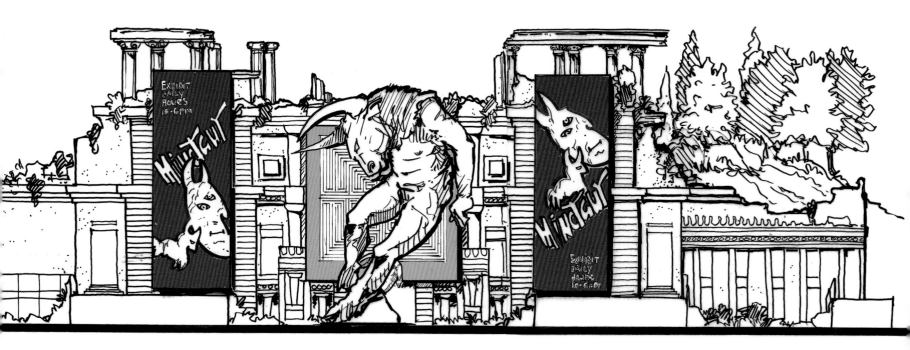

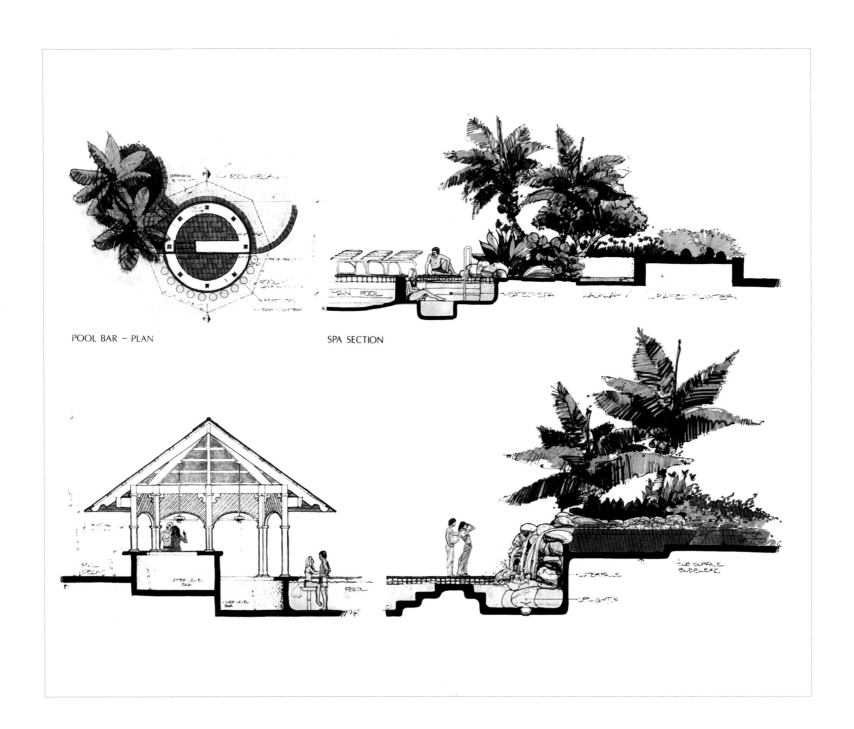

POOL BAR – PLAN

SPA SECTION

Line + Mark

71

Plants have a function of dividing the space.
Top: *Line + Mark*
Below: *Line + Mark + Color pencil*

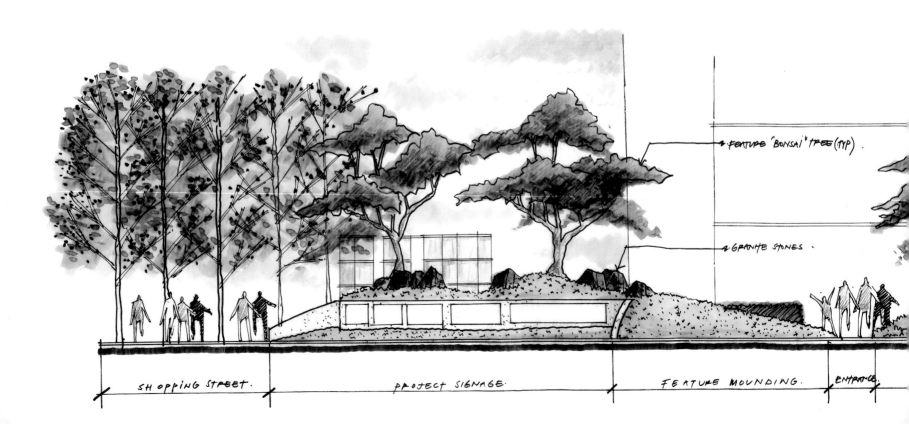

FEATURE "BONSAI" TREE (TYP).

GRANITE STONES.

SHOPPING STREET.   PROJECT SIGNAGE.   FEATURE MOUNDING.   ENTRANCE.

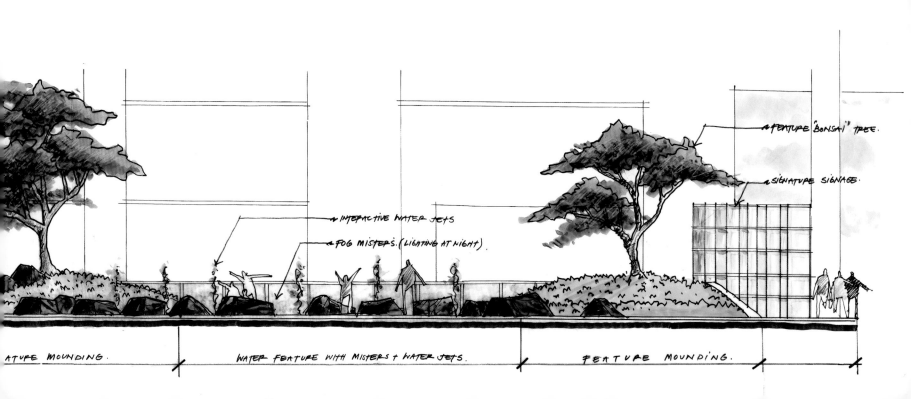

FEATURE "BONSAI" TREE.

SIGNATURE SIGNAGE.

INTERACTIVE WATER JETS

FOG MISTERS. (LIGHTING AT NIGHT)

ATURE MOUNDING.   WATER FEATURE WITH MISTERS ↑ WATER JETS.   FEATURE MOUNDING.

60CM

CONCRETE WALL W/
STUCCO FINISH

DECORATIVE POTS

SPECIAL PAVING

Left: It expresses the relationship of scale between walls
human scale and the surrounding plants
Line
Top right: Theme park scene
Line + Mark
Lower: The facade herein shows the relationship between
the building and the site
Line + Mark

GOLF COURSE

10m setback.

VIEWS TO GOLF.

PRIVATE TERRACE

RESIDENTIAL UNIT

ENTRY COURT

DRIVE & PARKING

GARAGES WITH STORAGE

Top: *Line + Mark*
Top right : *Line + Mark*
Right : It is convenient to deduce the design of the waterfront based on this picture.
Line + Mark

76

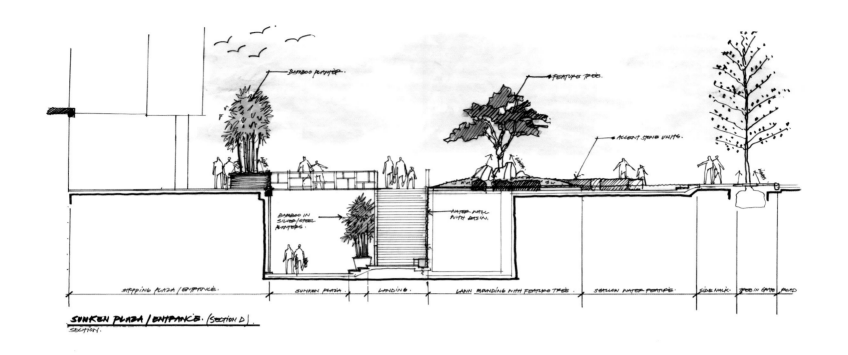

BAMBOO PLANTER.

FEATURE TREE.

ACCENT STONE UNITS.

BAMBOO IN
SILVER/STEEL
PLANTERS.

WATER WALL
WITH BASIN.

| SHOPPING PLAZA / ENTRANCE. | SUNKEN PLAZA | LANDING. | LAWN MOUNDING WITH FEATURE TREE | SHALLOW WATER FEATURE. | SIDEWALK. | TREE IN GRATE | ROAD |

SUNKEN PLAZA / ENTRANCE. (SECTION D)
SECTION.

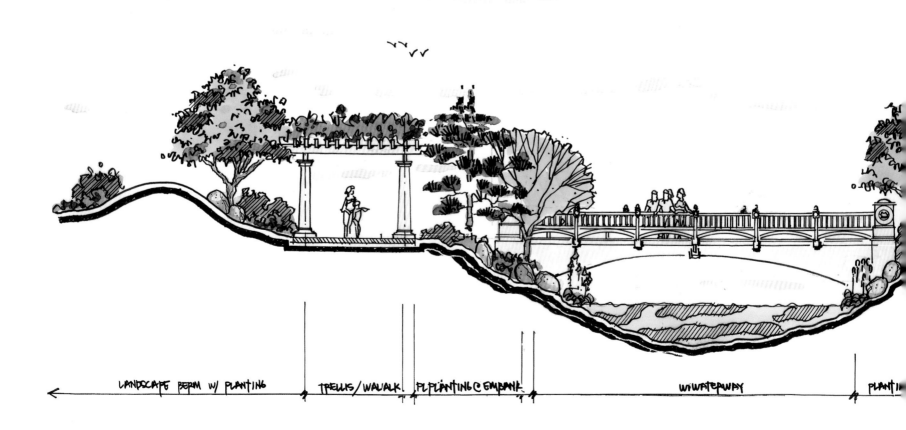

| LANDSCAPE BERM W/ PLANTING | TRELLIS / WALK. | PLANTING @ EMBANK. | W/WATERWAY | PLANT |

Left: *Line + Mark*
Top right: *Line + Mark*
lower: The facade view of the entry building of the theme
park, the slightly unskillful painting technique herein nicely
shows the features of the ancient architecture.
Line + Mark

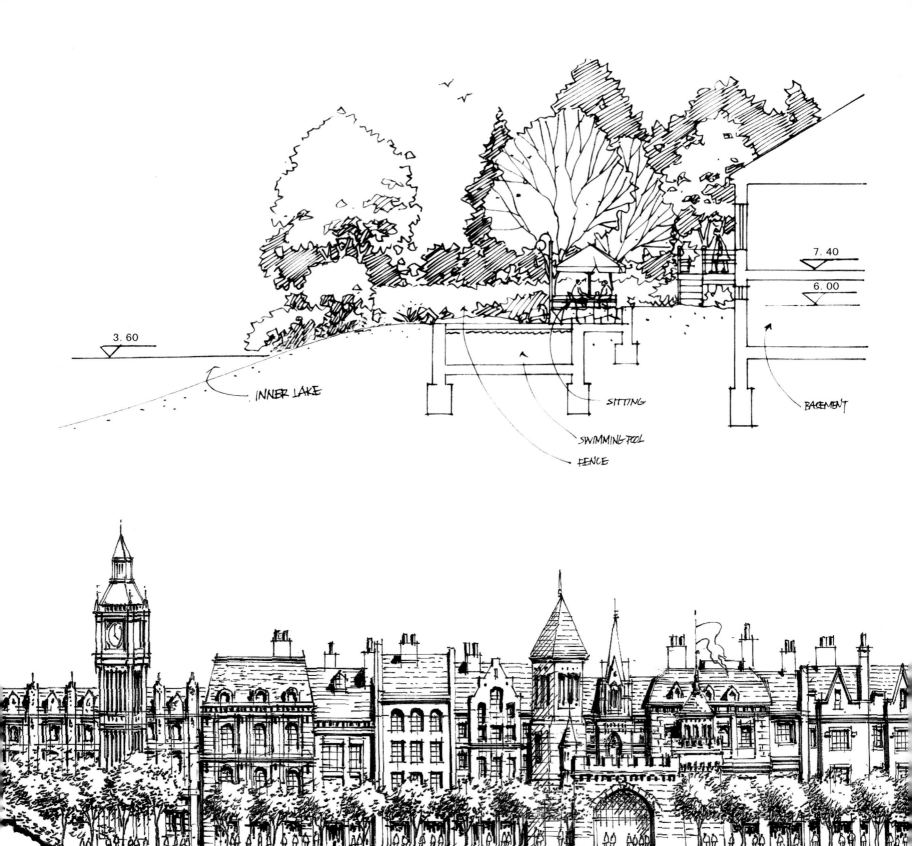

7. 40

6. 00

3. 60

INNER LAKE

SITTING

SWIMMING POOL

FENCE

BASEMENT

15 m

0 1 2 5m

Top left: The picture and the accompanying assay herein
are capable of accurately delivering the information.
Line
Lower left: SourthChina Mall London region facade. the
elaboration to architecture is punctilious, and the details
are finely portrayed, which both deserves to be learned.
Line
Right: *Line + Mark*

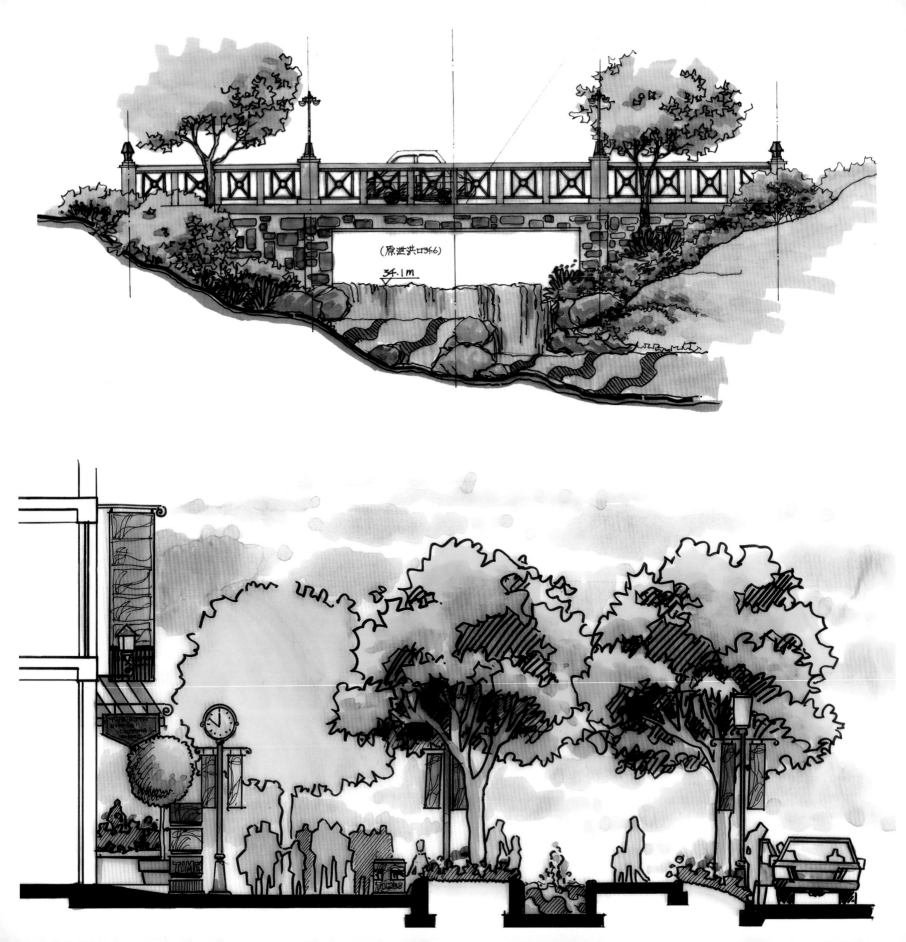

（原泄洪口34.6）

34.1m

Line + Mark

Top: It delicates a living scene while expressing the details.
Line + Mark

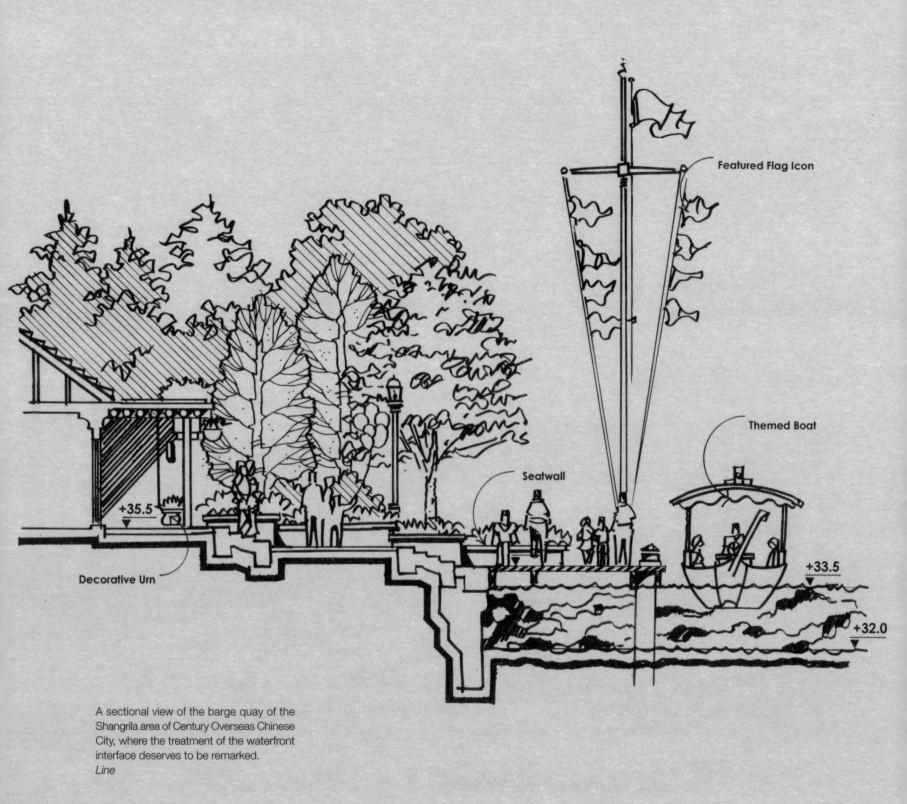

Featured Flag Icon

Themed Boat

Seatwall

+35.5

+33.5

+32.0

Decorative Urn

A sectional view of the barge quay of the
Shangrila area of Century Overseas Chinese
City, where the treatment of the waterfront
interface deserves to be remarked.
Line

+35.5

A sectional view of the barge quay of the
Shanghla area of Century Overseas Chinese
City, where the treatment of the waterfront
interface deserves to be remarked.
Line

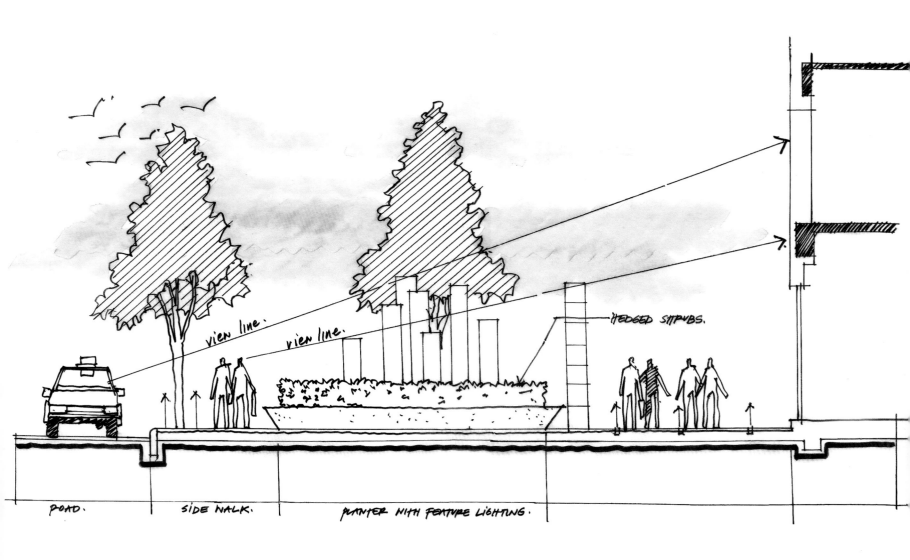

view line.

view line.

HEDGED SHRUBS.

ROAD.   SIDE WALK.   PLANTER WITH FEATURE LIGHTING.

Top: The brushwork herein is simple but accurate, without any superfluous things, and it delivers a message, that is, "pattern language" is a tool, the purpose of which is to express the intention of the design.
Line + Mark

Landscape Backdrop

Acrobatic Structures

Outdoor Dining

Bamboo Planting | Rollercoaster | Landscape Berm w/ Planting | Acrobatic Viewing Plaza | Acrobatic Viewing Plaza | Main Pedestrian Path

Low Planting | Lake | Rollercoaster Queue | Planting

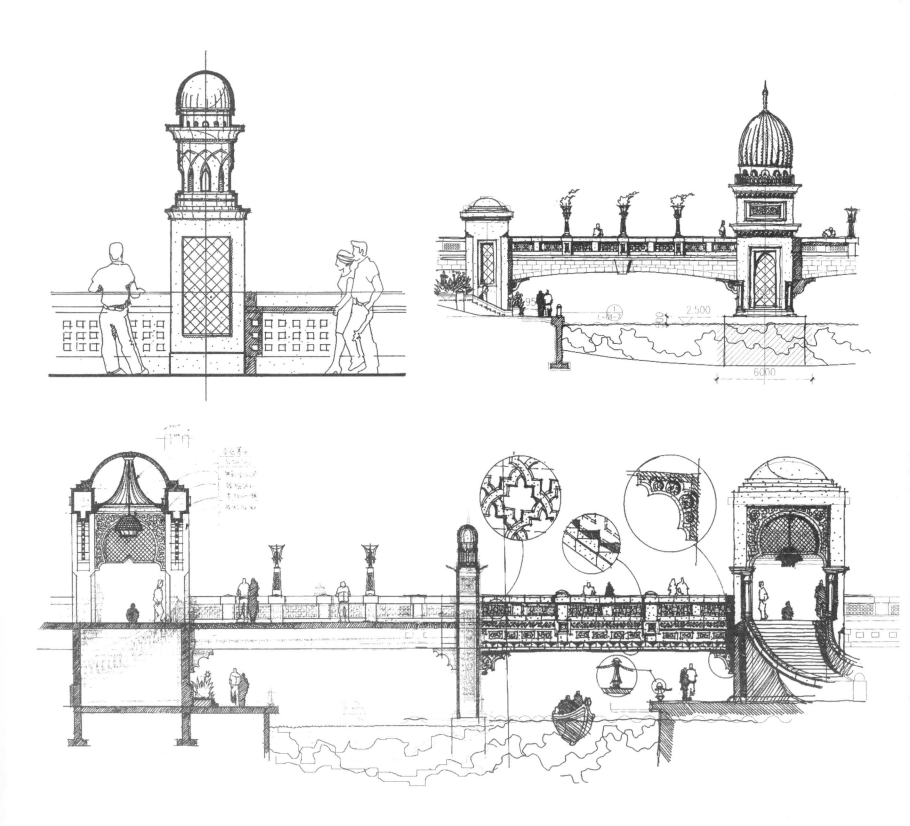

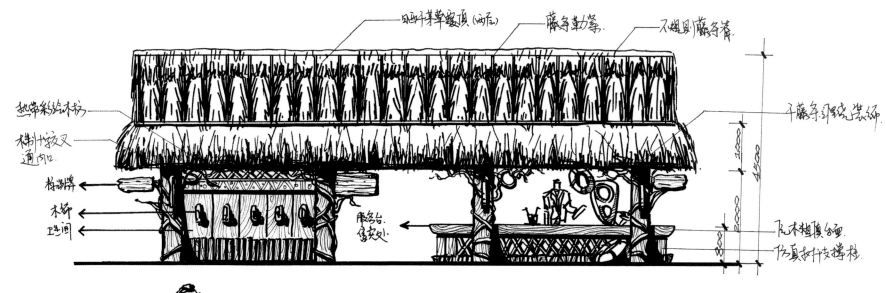

马西科茅草篷顶(两层)
藤条勒紧.
不规则藤条脊.

热带彩绘木板

木制枝叉
通风口

千藤条编织装饰.

枯树牌
木雕
卫生间

服务台.
售卖处.

仿木翘顶勾画
仿真扣件支撑柱.

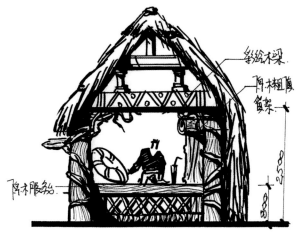

彩绘木梁.

仿木翘顶
货架.

原木服务.

Left: *Line*
Right: *Line + Mark*

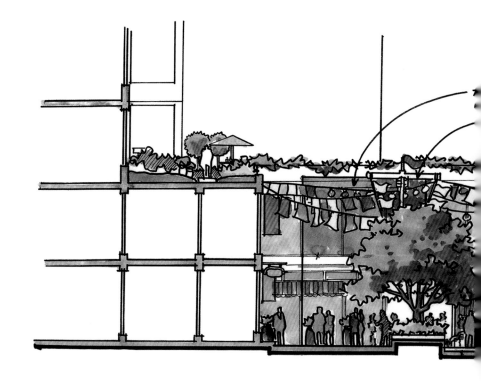

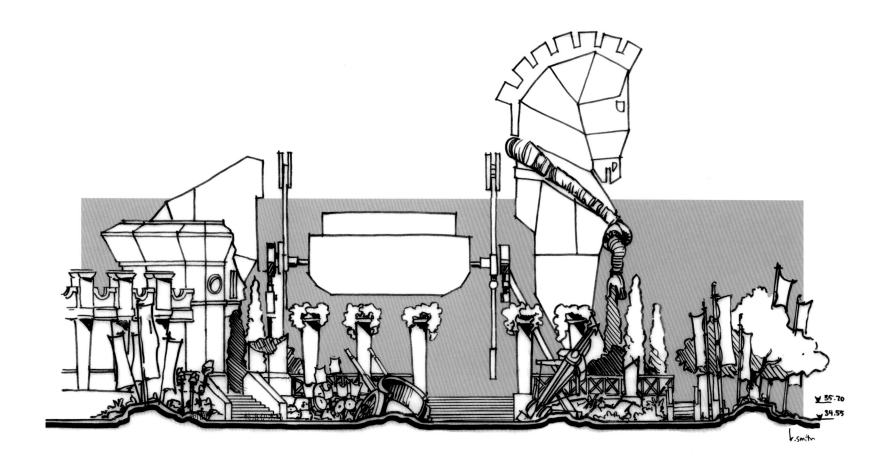

¥ 35.70
¥ 34.55

k.smith

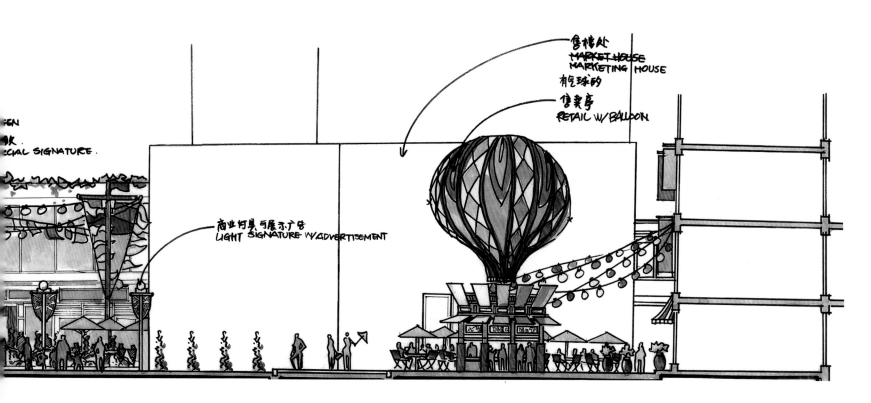

售楼处
MARKET HOUSE
MARKETING HOUSE

有气球的
售卖亭
RETAIL W/BALLOON

商业灯具可展示广告
LIGHT SIGNATURE W/ADVERTISEMENT

GEN

CIAL SIGNATURE.

Left: *Line + Mark*
Top right: *Line + Mark*
Right: *Line + Mark*

柱廊

水吧

海盗船

0 1 2   4M.

102

A facade view of the club entry: abundant plant stratification endows inspiration to the whole picture, and the use of shadow provides the building with volume sensation.
Line + Mark

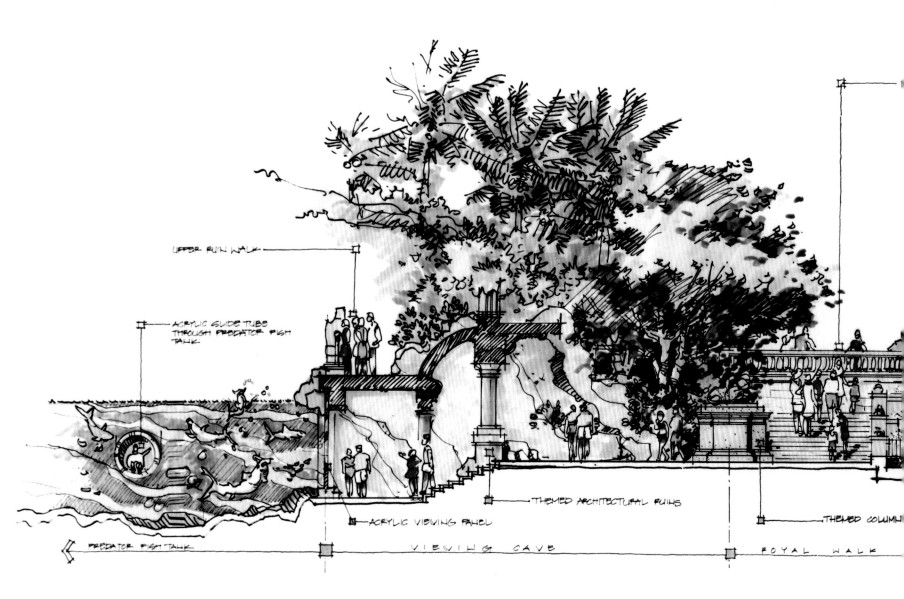

UPPER RUIN WALK

ACRYLIC GUIDE TUBE
THROUGH PREDATOR FISH
TANK

THEMED ARCHITECTURAL RUINS

ACRYLIC VIEWING PANEL

THEMED COLUMN

PREDATOR FISH TANK   VIEWING CAVE   ROYAL WALK

104

OLOOK AREA

STEPED WATER FEATURE

LUSH TROPICAL W/
ROCK AND WATER-SCAPE

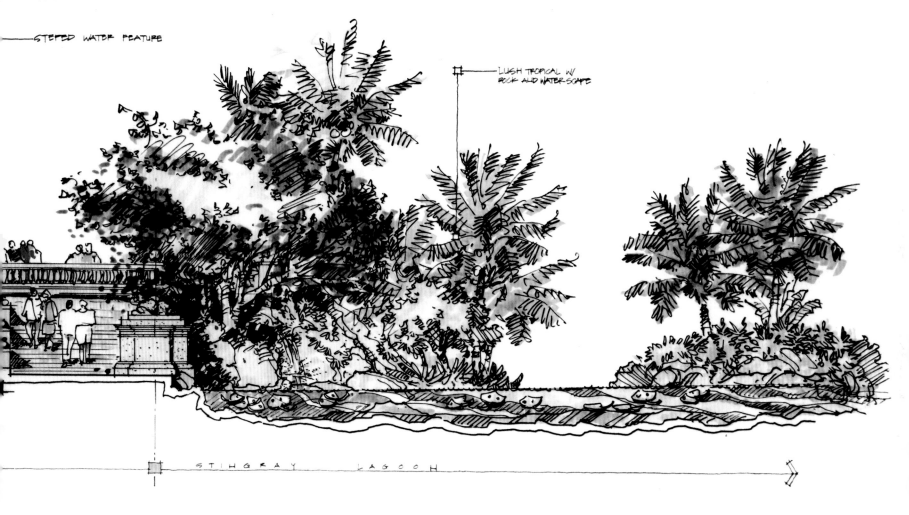

STINGRAY LAGOON

The structure of the building is very strict, the use of a large number of highsounding and cracked lines of the plants make the whole picture rich in comparative tension. The technique herein is skillful, and the picture is expressive.
Line + Mark

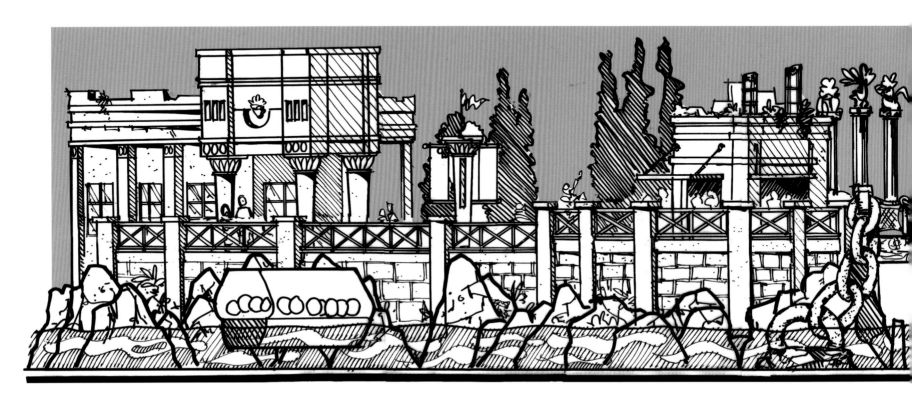

Top: *Line + Mark*
Below: A facade view of the waterfront landscape of theme park. It pays attention to lines of the treatment of details and shades to emphasize the space stratification.
Ink line + compute treatment

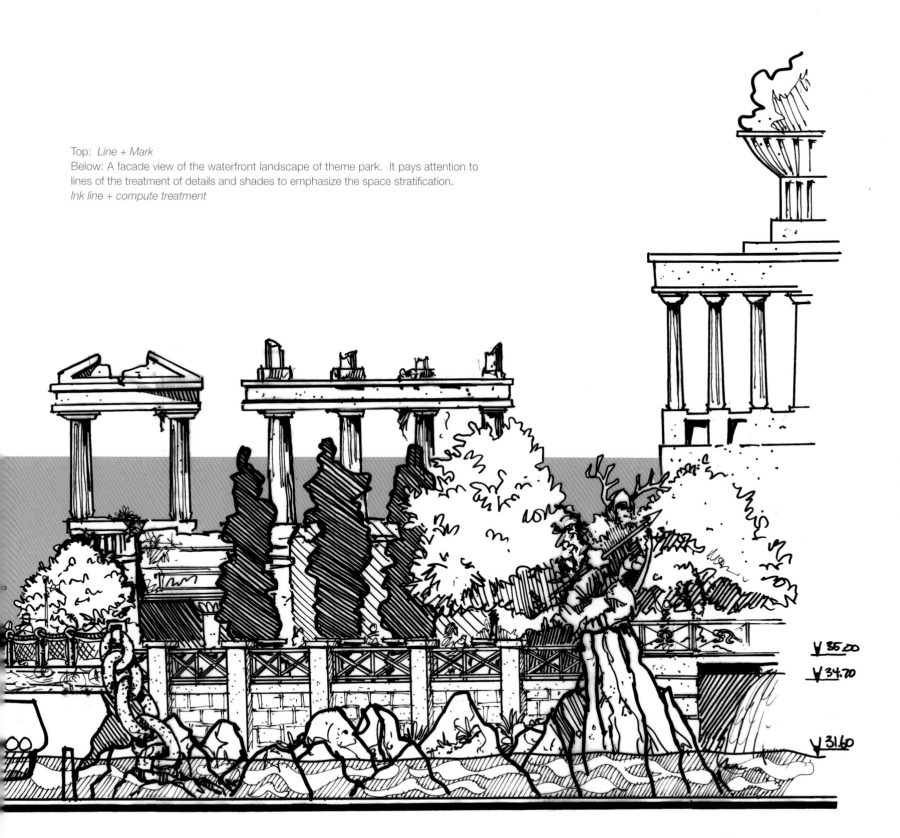

∀ 35.00

∀ 34.70

∀ 31.60

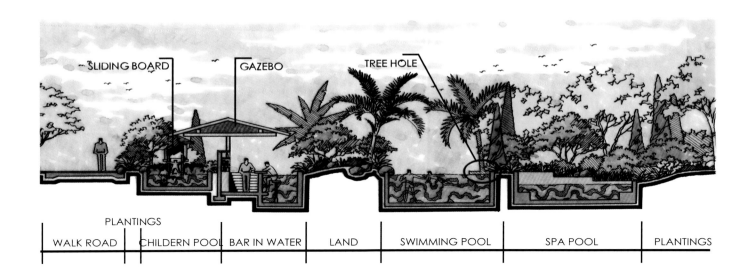

SLIDING BOARD   GAZEBO   TREE HOLE

PLANTINGS

| WALK ROAD | CHILDERN POOL | BAR IN WATER | LAND | SWIMMING POOL | SPA POOL | PLANTINGS |

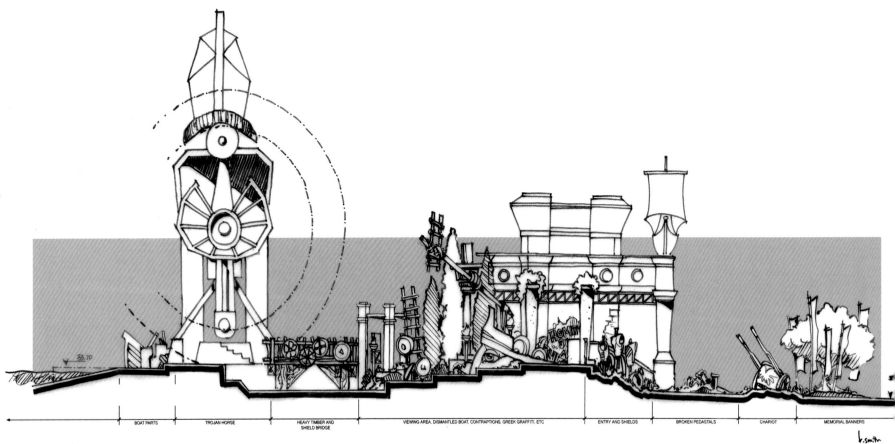

| BOAT PARTS | TROJAN HORSE | HEAVY TIMBER AND SHIELD BRIDGE | VIEWING AREA, DISMANTLED BOAT, CONTRAPTIONS, GREEK GRAFFITI, ETC | ENTRY AND SHIELDS | BROKEN PEDASTALS | CHARIOT | MEMORIAL BANNERS |

k.smith

ELEVATION B   VIEWING DECK

SCALE = 1:100

0   10   20   40   80

ARCADE

ARCADE BEYOND

RESIDENTIAL.

RESIDENTIAL.

ARCADE RETAIL

4 M.

5 M.

5 M.

20 METER DRAIN RESERVE
30 METER R.O.W.

Top left: club central environment
Line + Mark
Lower left: *line + compute treatment*
Right: Theme park scene
Line + Mark

Left: The type matter herein adds more
information to the picture.
Line + Mark
Right: *Line + Mark*

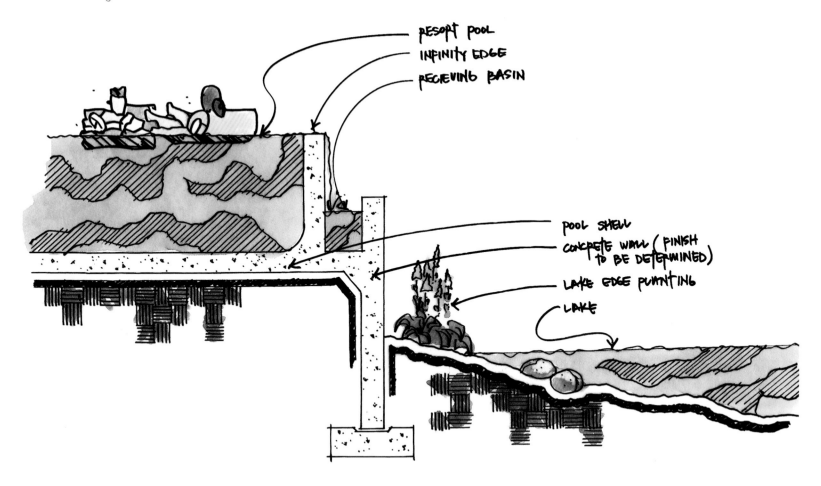

RESORT POOL

INFINITY EDGE

RECIEVING BASIN

POOL SHELL

CONCRETE WALL (FINISH
TO BE DETERMINED)

LAKE EDGE PLANTING

LAKE

62.25

61.45

61.55

61.75

61.25

60.55

0   0.5   1   2   3 (M)

61.45

61.75

61.75

61.45

60.85

60.25

60.00

111

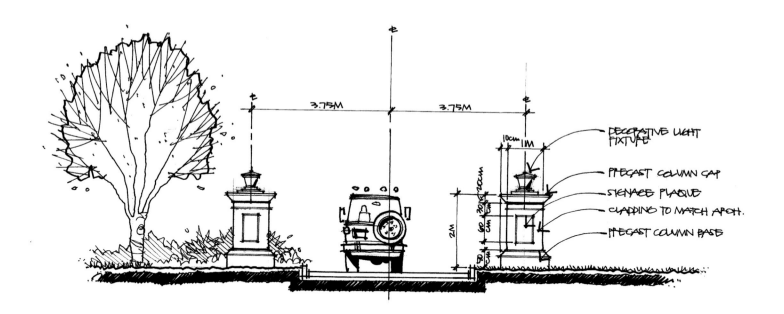

DECORATIVE LIGHT FIXTURE

PRECAST COLUMN CAP

SIGNAGE PLAQUE

CLADDING TO MATCH ARCH.

PRECAST COLUMN BASE

3.75M   3.75M

10cm 1M

2M

Top left: *Line*
Top right: *Line + Mark*
Below: *Line + Mark*

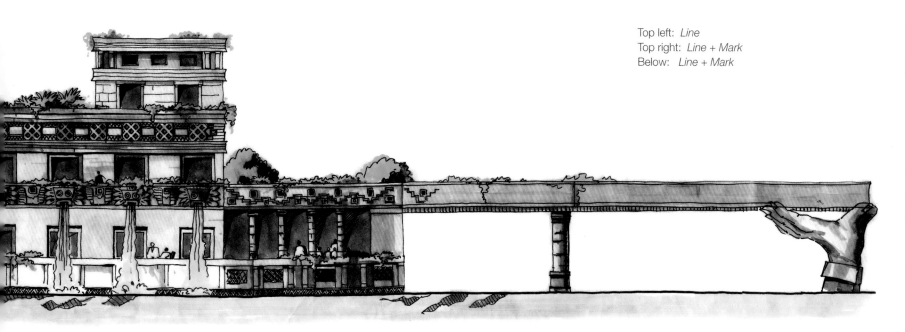

113

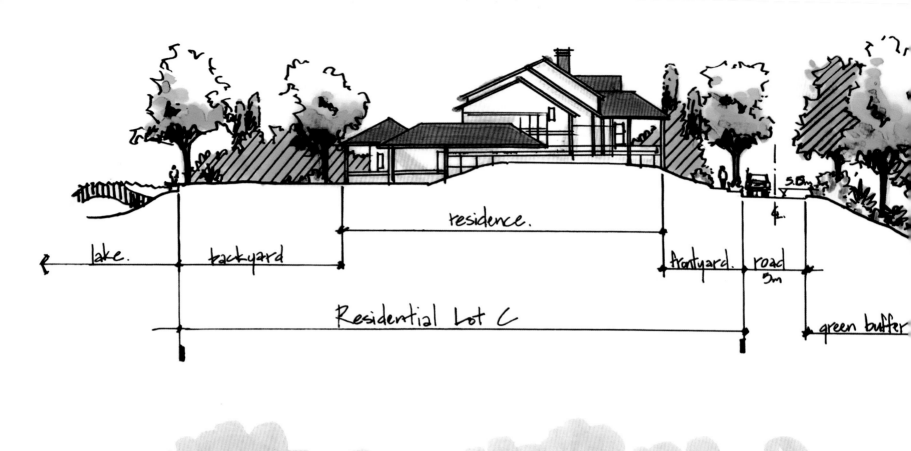

residence.

lake.   backyard

frontyard.   road
5m

5.0m

Residential Lot C

green buffer

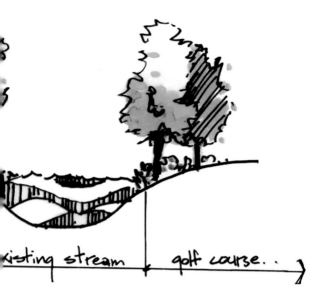

isting stream | golf course..

Line + Mark

117

E D S A (Asian)

Perspective View

Future Holliday Garden: *Line + Mark + computer treatment+ Color pencil*

Line + Mark + Color pencil

D. ZHANG

122

Line + Mark

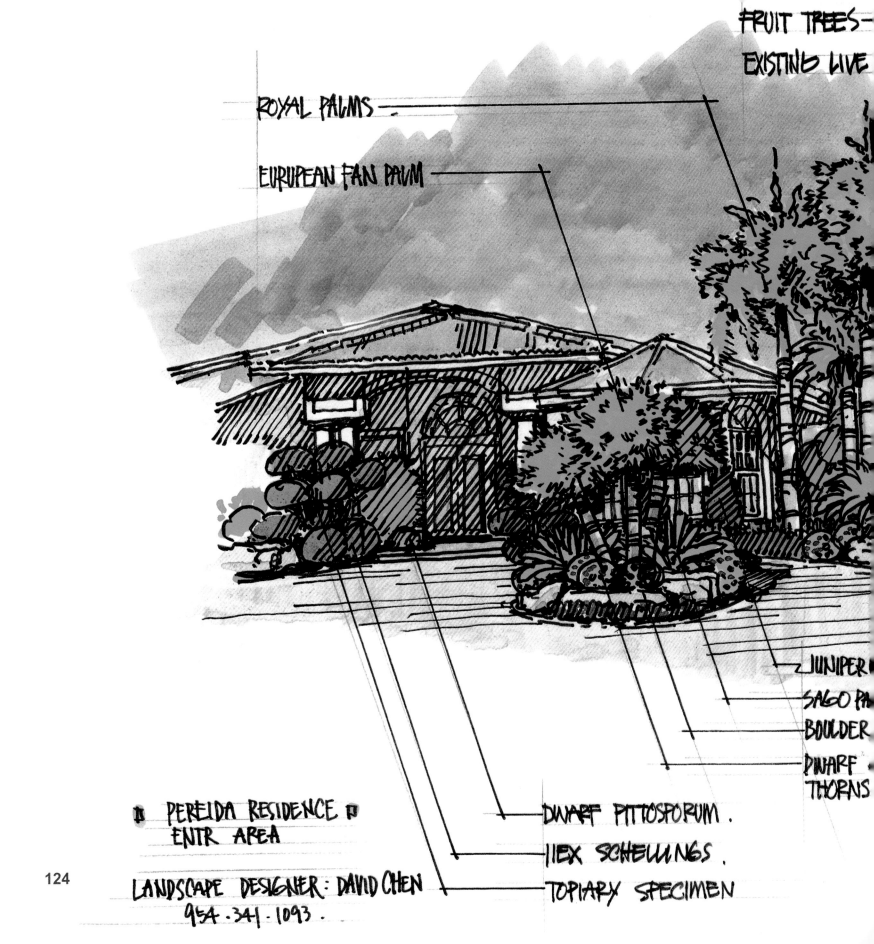

FRUIT TREES—

EXISTING LIVE

ROYAL PALMS

EUROPEAN FAN PALM

JUNIPER

SAGO PA

BOULDER

DWARF

THORNS

DWARF PITTOSPORUM.

ILEX SCHELLINGS.

TOPIARY SPECIMEN

PERELDA RESIDENCE
ENTR AREA

124

LANDSCAPE DESIGNER: DAVID CHEN
954·341·1093.

O REMAIN

(SA)

OF

The sense of the sketch is to directly express the meaning of the designer. This picture outlines a distal road, which is considered as public space psychologically attributing to personal.
Line + Mark

SAGO PALM.

SIM. BOULDER.

ANNUALS.

DWARF CROWN OF THORNS.

PYGMY DATE PALM

Line + Mark

Line + Mark

Skillful lines are used to accurately express the style of each designing components and the relationship between each other. The extent of colouring herein is also just appropriate.
Line + Mark

Line + Mark

134

Line + Mark

137

Bright color, forceful comparison, clear clew, and evident stratification, which provide a strong visual impact, are suitable for expression of the programming of landscape.
Line + Mark

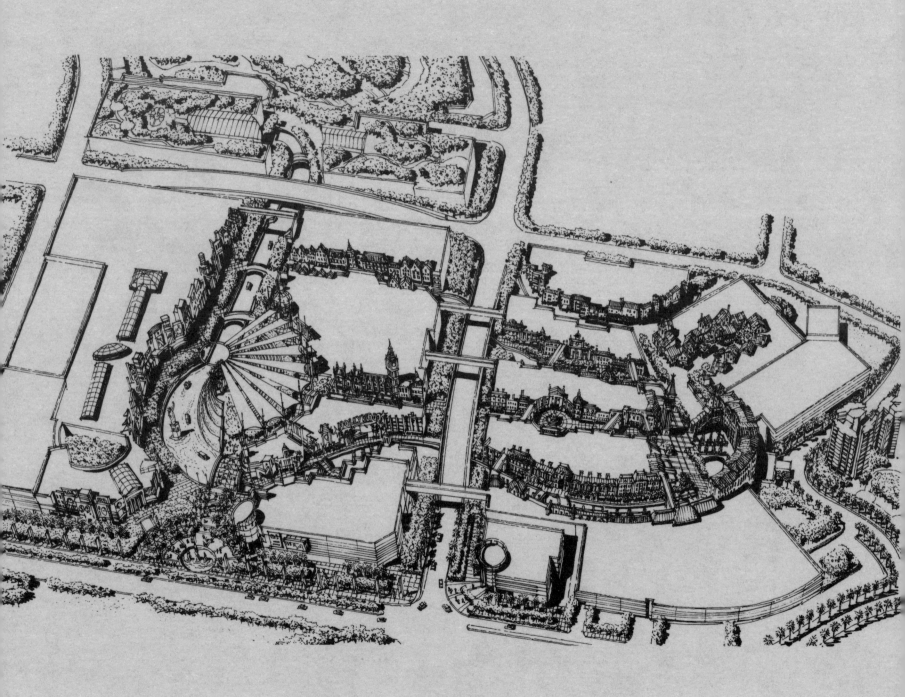

Line + Mark

Audacious lines are used in this picture to accurately draw a large-scale waterfront space. The purpose of selecting an angle of sight slightly higher than that of human is to express the spatial structure much more complete. The deuteric computer processing uses variations in light and shades not only to enrich the spatial stratification but also endows the picture with metallic modern atmosphere.
Line + computer treatment

142

Xi'an Ziwei: The rosiness and light vine black provide the picture with a
romantic or secretive atmosphere.
Line + Color pencil

Left: The white flower, by using alteration liquid, after colouring,
becomes living elements.
Line + Color pencil
Right: Luneng Center, Midpoint of Water.
Line + Mark + Color pencil

CENTER PLAZA. Z.D.

2002.8.

Left: San Francisco. The freehand style herein provides this picture with
strong artistry atmosphere
Line + Mark
Right: *Line + Mark*

Free lines and colors are much more advantageous to clearly
express the clew the designer.
Line + Mark

156

Left: *Line + Mark*
Right: The composition of the picture is strict, the lines are living and the whole picture has a strong decoration interest, which reflect the super technique and the profound art culture of the designer.
Line + Mark

The brushwork, like icon, is provided with a little bit of childness and a little bit of unruliness, and it is in pursuit of a decorational style.
Line + Mark

158

Line

162

D.CHEN . 97.

Line + Mark

165

Line + Mark

167

Below: The seemingly unorderly lines accurately express the scale of space and the use properties, which shows the clear clew and supper technique of the designer.
Line + Mark
Right: *Line + Mark*

The free and neat lines and vivid color herein make
the whole picture very natural.
Line + Mark

Left: *Line + Mark*
Right: The composition of the picture is strict
Line + Mark

173

Line + Mark

174

Line + Mark

Left: Chaoyang Ecologic Restaurant
Line + Mark
Right: *Line + Mark*

179

Left: *Line + Mark*
Right: Westlake park
Line + Mark

Line + Mark

Line + Mark

185

Left: *Line + Mark*
Right: The use of an axonometric drawing can effectively
control the morphological structure of the space
Line + Mark

Left: *Line + Mark*
Right: The use of sketch brushwork can rapidly express the meaning of design and carry out effective communication thereunder.
Line + Mark

Left: The effective view obtained by using photos with some options can nicely reflect the landscape and the environment.
Line + Mark
Right: *Line + Mark*

The brushwork is skillful, and the green-blue fundmenal tone is rich in romantic atmosphere. Meanwhile, the rest platform, the swimming pool and the plants are organized in a very smooth manner.
Line + Mark

Left: The note in the sketch not only useful for the designer to examining his work at any moment, but also makes his work much more persuasive.
Line + Mark
Right: *Line + Mark*

194

Line + Mark

Left: It is a well-protracted picture, where the designer uses various techniques, loose
or strict, to provide the picture with rhythm, but without losing harmonization.
Line + Mark
Right: *Line + Mark*

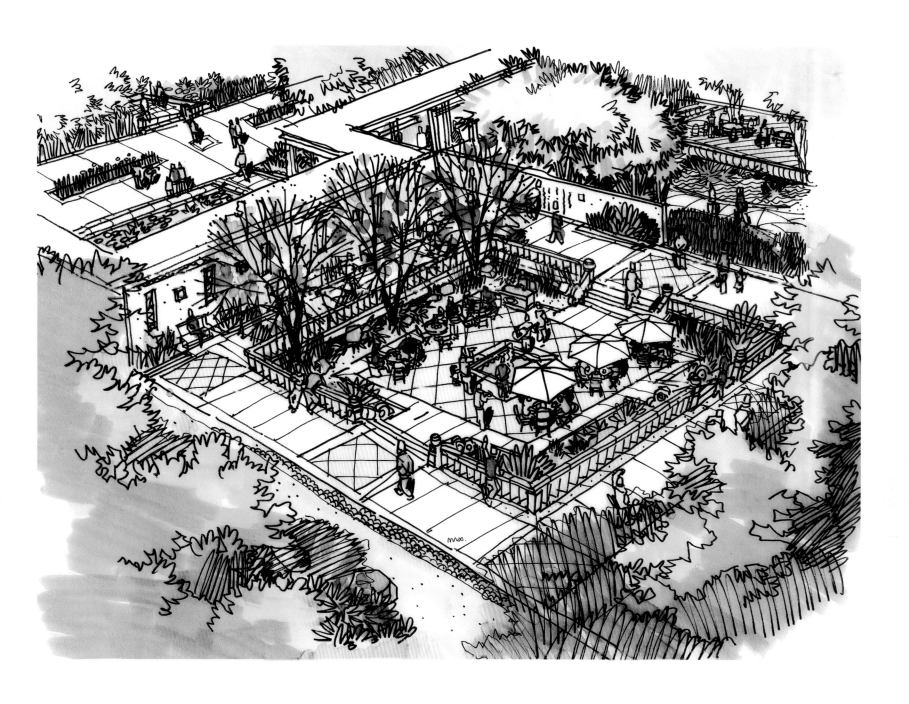

Left: Jindu Huafu
Line + Mark
Right: *Line + Mark*

There are two different sets of color in the same picture of black and white lines, so
that they brings about different interests: from warmth under the fluorescent lamp
to impassion under the lamplight in the evening.
Line + Mark

A few lines drawn by pen are used to be compared with a large scale of color blocks, and the complex programming herein is generalized. Moreover, the compact district is detailedly described. The uppermost oblique lines successfully immaterialize the background and brighten the main body.
Line + Mark

Line + Mark

Line + Mark

212

Xiangshui bay: These two pictures use modern drawing
techniques. Buddhist sense is created from the white cloud,
blue water, and the green hills, and the non-smooth brushwork
herein express a desire and pursuit of truth.
Line + Mark

215

216

Left: An aeroview of the golf villas, Westlake Nandu.
Line + Mark
Right: *Line + Mark*

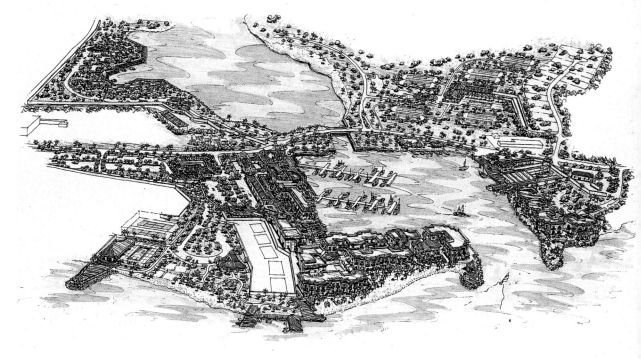

Left: Venice. A manner close to collage is used to treat the relationship among buildings and between building and landscape, to reflect the mussy but busy modern commercial space.
Line + Mark
Right: *Line + Mark*

ZANDT. 2002·10·7

As sketch, it is provided with very high design technique. One-point perspective makes the sectional view much more persuasive, and the details therefor are also very conspicuous.
Line + Mark

221

Line + Mark

The designer herein expresses as many as possible elements in the limited picture. The human activities, such as leisure, tour, entertainment and consumption, are realized through the space created by landscape design, wherein there are a lot of detailed design deserve to be learned.
Line + Mark

225

Line + Mark

ORCHID

229

231

GZL 2003.12.7.

233

234

Left: *Line*
Right: *Line + Mark*

235

Line + Mark

242

Left: Hotspring
Line + Mark
Right: *Line + Mark*

244

ZANDT. 30/10/02.

245

Left: fountain
Line + Mark
Right: *Line+ Mark*

247

We believe that the real
landscape architects and
the best architects are earth-connected
they are the planters...
the farmers...
the explorers...
the writers...
who create new markets
and shape styles, and
the root and reroot
in the region wherever
they work.

wolong panda reserve
Sichuan province PRC
March 1st 2003
MCL.

materials 1.

Line + Mark

Left: *Line + Mark*
Right: Tianjin Sunco
Line + Mark

Left: Dodgem sign(parergon)
Line + Mark
Right: *Line + Mark*

Left: *Line + Water-color*
Right: The sketch in trip correspondingly requires a lower level of technique. It is an fundamental purpose to directly hit the point and express an accurate space relationship.
Line

259

Line + Mark

Left: *Line + Mark*
Right: Courtyard
Line + Mark

Xiangshui bay
Line + Mark

Baby Panda Enclosure.
Panda Research center
chengdu, china
MCN · 02.23.07.

Left: Parergon
Line + Mark
Right: *Line + Mark*

Left: *Line + Color pencil*
Right: *Line + Mark*

Line + Mark

272

Road landscape of villas: a full-bodied American-style fallow scene.
Line + Mark

Ecologic swimming pool
Line + Mark

277

Left: A large scale of bice impression is used herein to make
the deep and serene situation stand out, and the spatial structure of each fallow regions are also expressed very clearly.
Line + Mark
Right top, Right lower: *Line + Mark*

Jindu huafu zhi Hefeng
Line + Mark

EDSA one of the world's leading planning, landscape and architecture design firms since founded in 1960. With the seven offices in Fort Lauderdale, Washington, Orlando, Los Angeles, Provo, Buenos Aires, and Beijing, we have the resources to provide pre-development project management, complete planning and design, and field supervision services all over the world.

EDSA(Asian), a joint venture company in Beijing, China, which now employs about 150 staff including 120 professionals. David Chen is the president and chief designer of the company, he is responsible for the management of the company and setting the design standards for the company's portfolios of projects. Our expert staff of planners, landscape architects, architects, engineers and support personnel from abroad and domestic provides the highest quality of services including Environmental Planning & Ecotourism, Large Mix-use Development Projects, Urban Commercial & Public Open Space, Community Planning & Design, Attractions & Entertainment, and Hotels & Resorts. The firm's work has been recognized with numerous awards for design and planning excellence and environmental sensitivity. More importantly, the successful designs and planning of project have been enjoyed by people who experience them such as real estate developers, owners and Chinese government.